THE KILLING
SPREE

BOOKS BY ANITA PADDOCK

Blind Rage

Closing Time

Cold Blooded

The Killing Spree

THE KILLING SPREE

A True Story of a String of Brutal Murders, Rapes, and the Cop Who Tried to Stop It

By Anita Paddock

First Edition
ISBN: 978-1-68313-245-5
Library of Congress Control Number: 2022950885
Printed and bound in the U.S.A.

Pen-L Publishing
Fayetteville, Arkansas
www.Pen-L.com

For Doug and Jan Kelley

Contents

Chapter One 1

Chapter Two 8

Chapter Three 12

Chapter Four 16

Chapter Five 18

Chapter Six 20

Chapter Seven 23

Chapter Eight 25

Chapter Nine 27

Chapter Ten 33

Chapter Eleven 35

Chapter Twelve 38

Chapter Thirteen 41

Chapter Fourteen 47

Chapter Fifteen 50

Chapter Sixteen 52

Chapter Seventeen 54

Chapter Eighteen 56

Chapter Nineteen 63

Chapter Twenty 65

Chapter Twenty-One 69

Chapter Twenty-Two 72

Chapter Twenty-Three 76

Chapter Twenty-Four 79

Chapter Twenty-Five 84

Chapter Twenty-Six 88

Chapter Twenty-Seven 92

Chapter Twenty-Eight 102

Chapter Twenty-Nine 106

Chapter Thirty 118

Chapter Thirty-One 122

Chapter Thirty-Two 124

Chapter Thirty-Three 127

Chapter Thirty-Four 130

Chapter Thirty-Five 142

Chapter Thirty-Six 144

Chapter Thirty-Seven 147

Epilogue 149

Acknowledgements 152

About the Author 153

More books! 154

CHAPTER ONE
Randy Basnett
September 24, 1976

Randy Basnett was sitting on the living room couch when he scooped up his baby daughter, Amanda, out of her bassinet and gave her little kisses on her tummy. He couldn't believe that he could love a child as much as he did. He lay back on the couch and placed her on his tummy where their hearts beat as one.

His wife, Cindy, was in the kitchen preparing breakfast for Bill, who was four, and his sister, Shannon, who was two years older. They were Cindy's by a previous marriage. Randy had wanted to adopt them, but the natural father won the court battle. Randy had hired an attorney, and he and Cindy had attended the court proceedings. She had cried, but Randy just got mad.

Cindy had first seen Randy when he responded to a call she had made to the police station in the middle of the night. Someone was trying to break in her car at the apartment complex where she and her children were living. It turned out to be a man who was drunk and had the wrong car. Officer Randy Basnett had said, "Sorry for your trouble. Nothing to worry about."

She had thought Randy was handsome, very, very handsome. Months later she saw him again. And then a few months later. Each time she saw him, her heart fluttered. Finally, he asked her for a date.

Cindy was a cute little thing, feisty and outspoken. They bought a small place in Barling, a little town outside of Fort Smith, Arkansas. Houses were cheaper in Barling, and it was a good place for young couples to buy their starter home.

"Just think," he told Cindy after the baby was born. "Isn't it wonderful, this mystery of life—that two people can share and produce a living thing."

Randy grew up in Fort Smith and attended all twelve years of school there. Handsome as a movie star, he could always get a date. He was very likable. He kept in contact with many of his friends from high school days.

Always good with numbers, he first tried working in accounting offices. But, he soon found out that he didn't like sitting in an office all day. He preferred being able to see the sky and feel the sun on his shoulders. He was an outdoors guy through and through.

At the age of thirty, Randy was in the profession he had always wanted to be in. He proudly wore the Fort Smith Police Department uniform. Confident and a little cocky, he was the kind of guy who liked to wear sunglasses.

Cindy's dad, Odell Davis, and Randy really hit it off, mainly because they both loved to fish. Odell had been in the military and had also been a Fort Smith detective until he retired because of ill health due to diabetes and heart trouble. He and his wife, Emogene, decided to sell their home on Harvard Avenue so they could fulfill their dream and move to Lake Tenkiller.

Tenkiller was constructed by damming part of the Illinois River. The lake had 13,000 acres of water and 130 miles of shoreline. Only sixty miles from Fort Smith, it was a favorite place to fish and water ski for folks in both Oklahoma and Arkansas. Lots of people retired there or had lake retreats where they lived in one of the many trailers that dotted the various lake communities.

The nearest town of any size was Tahlequah, the capitol of the Cherokee Nation. A college was also there. It was a pretty little town that attracted tourists as well as locals.

Cindy stood at the door between the living room and kitchen and for a moment, looked at the sweet scene on the couch.

Both father and daughter were sound asleep.

She poked his shoulder. "Randy, wake up. You might roll over and the baby would fall on the floor."

He looked up. "I was just resting my eyes."

She leaned over and kissed him on the lips. They stayed in an embrace until Amanda woke.

Cindy said, "I'll get her bottle and you can feed her while I clean up the kitchen."

"Okay. My shift starts at 11:15, so I'll have lots of time."

Cindy always felt a little pang of fright when Randy left for work. She never let it show though. She would always be a good policeman's wife like her mother was. Growing up as the daughter of a policeman had prepared her for this life.

Fort Smith police work could be dangerous, perhaps as dangerous as in any town in Arkansas. Fort Smith had a history of being a rough and tough town. It was once full of saloons, whore houses, and churches.

Its nickname was Hell on the Border, and for good reason. It had been the jumping off place to Indian Territory, where the Trail of Tears ended. American Indians had been sent on the terrible journey from the lush Southeast to the flat brown earth of the area the government designated as their new home.

This proved to be a good locale for criminals to hide out because there was no law in Indian Territory. Fort Smith was a place you passed through on the way to somewhere else: outlaws seeking freedom, trappers canoeing upriver, gold miners headed to California, and ranchers headed to Texas. Prostitution thrived on the streets close to the Arkansas River. One of the most famous whore houses belonged to Pearl Starr, the daughter of Belle Starr, a wild and woolly female criminal who lived in Indian Territory. She was known to be a fine horsewoman as well as a fine girlfriend to fine thieves.

The fort was first established by the U.S. government to keep peace between the Cherokees and Osage who lived on the border along the Arkansas River. But soon some semblance of law and order in Indian Territory was added to the job of Federal judges. They were tasked to employ U.S. Marshals who were sent out to capture the criminals and bring them back to Fort Smith to stand trial. Judge Isaac Parker was the most famous judge who meted out justice that was carried out by public hangings on the lawn of the Federal Courthouse. It was an event likened to today's State Fairs or Halloween carnivals. People bought tamales from an old Mexican who sold them out of a cart he pushed around. The rooming houses were always full with those who came for the hanging.

Randy Basnett loved the history of his home town. He saw the movie, True Grit, written by Charles Portis, who did much of his research at the Fort Smith Public Library.

Cindy returned to the living room with an eight-ounce bottle of formula in one hand and the morning newspaper in the other. Amanda readily accepted the bottle, and soon she was full and back asleep in her daddy's arms.

Randy laid her back in the bassinet. It had wheels on it, and Cindy could easily move it wherever she needed to.

Randy picked up the Southwest Times Record and read the Sports page first. He wanted to see who was playing whom in football that Friday night. Friday night football always stirred up a little trouble with a little beer drinking. Randy wasn't too old that he couldn't remember those days from his own high school experience.

Soon Bill and Shannon came running in and jumped on his lap. "Daddy Randy, read us the funny paper?"

"Okay. Let's see what old blind Mr. McGoo is up to."

Later, when Randy was leaving for work, he kissed Cindy good bye. "Hey, honey, has your dad's house sold yet?

Cindy laughed. "Randy Basnett, you will be the first to know!"

Asking Cindy if her parents had sold their house was an everyday thing with Randy. He could not wait for his in-laws to move to Tenkiller, his favorite place on earth. It got to be a joke between Randy and Cindy.

Cindy also got along well with her in-laws. She and her three children frequently visited Peggy and Monroe Basnett. To Cindy's delight, they had welcomed her children into their hearts almost immediately.

They often went to visit Randy's grandpa, Deke Fant, just over the state line into Oklahoma at Muldrow. The children especially loved to see the pet squirrel come up and eat peanuts out of Grandpa Deke's hand.

Cindy and Randy enjoyed their family life. She was an only child, and Odell and Emogene were happy that their little girl had found such a good man to love and marry. Cindy was very religious and believed that it was God who granted a happy life to them.

Cindy remembered one night, early in their marriage, when her husband returned from an evening shift with his lip badly swollen.

"What in the world happened to you, honey?"

"I got a call to go to Sally Ann's, you know that quicky mart close to Northside High School? There was a drunk woman causing a disturbance. I tried to calm her down, and she cold-cocked me with a carton of bottled beer. Miller High Life, I believe. I never wanted to hit a woman before, but I came close tonight."

"The guys are going to tease you when they see that lip."

"Oh, yeah. I'm not going to tell them it was a woman though. And don't you tell anybody either."

Cindy knew her husband was liked by his peers, and they would razz him for days. He was a "man's man." That was one reason she loved him. One of many.

Randy Basnett, September 18, 1946 – September 24, 1976

CHAPTER TWO
September 17, 1976
ONE WEEK EARLIER

John Edward Swindler stepped off a Greyhound bus in Columbia, South Carolina. He walked inside the station, found the door that read M E N, and stayed long enough to see if there were any guys loitering around.

When he walked outside, under the blue South Carolina sky, he breathed deeply, but all he smelled was grease, smoke, and piss. He had forty dollars in his pocket, courtesy of the warden of Leavenworth. He'd been released on good behavior.

What a joke, Swindler thought. *That bastard just wanted to get rid of me.*

Swindler had been put in solitary, but he came out meaner than ever. He had never done any good behavior. He had often told fellow inmates, "My pappy taught me to take care of myself and not let nobody push me around."

He recalled shooting a neighbor's dog and nine goats. That was when he was nine or ten, and the justice of the peace had called it a childish prank, because he didn't know what to do with him.

He felt a hand on his shoulder. "Hi, Johnny, welcome home."

John Swindler looked up and down at his younger brother. He didn't like to be called Johnny.

"Hi, Robert. I see you got all duded up to welcome your baby brother home from Leavenworth."

Robert looked down at his khaki pants and tasseled loafers. "It's what I have to wear to work."

Robert couldn't help but compare himself to his brother who was tremendously fat, had long fuzzy red hair, and whose jowls resembled a hog who had just won a blue ribbon at the Richland County Fair.

"You work at a bank?" John laughed loudly at his own joke. "Does your fancy office buddies know you've got an ex-con for a brother?"

"Well, you know, Johnny, besides you, I've got three other brothers who are in prison, just got out, or fixing to be headed that way. And I don't work at a bank. I work at a computer business that works for banks."

"Why you here, anyway?"

Robert reached into his pants pocket for a folded piece of yellow paper. "I found you a place to stay. Seventeen dollars a month, and this is the address. Also my phone number. Call me in a few days about a job I've got lined up for you."

"Okay, and thanks. I guess thanks is what I ought to say. You forgotten I can't read?"

"Well, you can read what you want to, Johnny boy. I've got to get back to work. Keep in touch, Johnny boy. And maybe cut your hair and take a bath. Buy some clothes with the money the prison gave you."

John Edward Swindler watched his brother leave. He laughed and held up his middle finger. He took the yellow sheet of paper, wadded it up into a ball, and threw it toward a large metal trash can. "Two points," he yelled.

If someone mistreated him, John Edward Swindler took revenge. The revenge might consist of burning down someone's house, setting fire to a car, robbing a gas station, or stealing a car. He confessed to once tying a dude to a fire plug and then spraying him with lighter fluid. "I kept sticking matches to his chest," he bragged. "I told him I'd burn him alive."

He liked to talk about how mean he was.

His size and looks intimidated people. At six feet tall, he weighed close to three hundred pounds, had pimply skin, and a fat face. He let his fuzzy red hair grow long to further his frightening looks. Nobody in the confines of a prison dared refuse his sexual advances. If they did, Swindler beat them up so bad that they wished they had given in to him.

His brother was doing his good deed of the year, arranging a job for John.

Of course, Swindler didn't want a stinking job.

Swindler in Leavenworth mugshot in early 1976.

CHAPTER THREE

High school sweethearts Greg Bicknell and Dottie Rhodes had recently graduated from Columbia High School in Columbia, South Carolina. Both had summer jobs. She was working as a teacher in a dance studio that was near where her boyfriend worked at a hospital supply firm.

Greg was tall and lanky, and Dottie was short and only weighed a little over one hundred pounds. She was also taking part-time classes at a Bible college in Columbia.

Driving her father's car, a green 1972 Maverick, Dottie picked up her boyfriend and they went for lunch at a popular drive-in that specialized in old fashioned hamburgers wrapped in greasy waxed paper.

The couple had finished their hamburgers and were working on the Cherry Cokes they had ordered. Suddenly, a scary fat guy opened the passenger door, climbed in, and jabbed a gun into Greg's ribs.

"Do what I say and I won't hurt you."

Dottie started sobbing. She was not supposed to be driving the car anyplace other than to work and back home. Her daddy had already told her that she was seeing way too much of Greg, and he was limiting their contact to weekends only. He didn't want anything to disrupt her plans to attend the University of South Carolina.

"Daddy's going to kill me," Dottie whispered to Greg.

Greg tried to reason with the man. "Please, mister. My girlfriend doesn't have any money and neither do I. This is her dad's car."

Swindler said, "You know where Forrest Hill's fishing lake is, girlie?"

Dottie nodded her head yes. She had begun to cry, and her tears had quickly washed trails down her face.

"Well, drive there and be quick about it. I ain't got all day."

Dottie drove as fast as she could. She hoped a cop might stop her for speeding, but she didn't see a single black and white car.

"How much gas you got?"

"About half a tank," Dottie said.

When they got to the lake area, it was deserted of cars. Swindler told the couple to walk toward the woods that were full of pin oaks and palmetto trees.

Greg and Dottie were good kids. They might have been called nerds, and neither one had ever disappointed their parents. They were just two kids who loved each other and complemented one another.

Greg was afraid that the man would rape Dottie, but it soon became apparent to Greg that, by the leers aimed his way, he was the one this apish-looking man was interested in.

The man told Greg to take off his denim overalls, and as Greg was folding them the way he did every night before going to bed, Greg was pushed violently down over a fallen tree that lay on the sandy soil. Swindler pulled off Greg's Jockey underwear and briefly held them under his nose. Then he dropped his pants (he was not wearing underwear) and proceeded to sodomize Greg.

Greg screamed out in pain at the indecent act this man was performing on him, especially in front of Dottie. Greg could feel what he thought must be blood on his upper thighs.

"Oh, you're a virgin, pretty boy."

Greg looked toward Dottie who was screaming for the man to stop. "You will go to hell for this!" she yelled.

"Shut up, little skinny missy, or you'll be next."

Greg was in such pain that he could barely whisper. "Don't hurt her, mister. Please don't hurt her."

"Just make her shut the fuck up, and I'll let the both of you go home to your mommies."

Dottie tried her best to stop crying, but she was more frightened than she'd ever been in her life. She kept on sobbing, loud gulps of tears. She tried to pray the prayer her grandmother taught her: Now I lay me down to sleep ...

The noonday sun was beating down on Greg's bare skin. Swindler had also ripped off Greg's shirt, ridiculing his victim's white chest as he tore the cloth. Part of the excitement of the rape encompassed ridicule.

John Edward Swindler had been out of Leavenworth two days.

Later that day, a policeman found a woman's purse in a drainage ditch by an elementary school in an area of Columbia known as Forest Acres. According to a driver's license and a checkbook inside, the purse belonged to Dottie Rhodes. The purse didn't appear to have been in the ditch long, so the policeman thought it had only been lost a short time. He called the telephone number on her checks, and her family reported that she hadn't returned home with her father's car.

When Greg didn't come home, his father drove to his place of work and found Greg's car in the otherwise empty parking lot. Both sets of parents were frantic. Neither child would be late coming home without calling first. Their disappearance was soon on radio and television news casts. Police pleaded with the public to be on the lookout for the green Maverick belonging to Dottie's dad.

Within twenty-four hours, the police received a call from a fisherman who had spotted the green Maverick. The police investigated. They could not find the car but, continuing the search, they arrived at a horrible scene.

Greg was tied to a tree trunk, nude. Dottie, fully clothed, was lying on the ground with her leg tied to a tree limb. They had each been shot twice in the head.

It was a sight that policemen never get used to. "Who would do this just to steal a car?" asked one of the younger guys.

He was answered by an older and more cynical officer, "A real savage. I feel sorry for the man who tries to arrest him."

CHAPTER FOUR

A couple of days later, Swindler went downtown to a bar, and sat down next to a guy he recognized. Swindler ordered a beer and, while he was slugging it down, the guy whispered to Swindler that the cops were accusing him of the murder of a young couple.

"Who told you that?" Swindler asked. He and the bearer of bad news had done time together, but they weren't pals.

"Don't know the guy. Just somebody I sat next to at a bar."

Swindler slid off the barstool, dropped a dollar on the bar, and left. He rushed down the sidewalk until he found a phone booth. He put a coin in the slot and asked to be connected to the Columbia Police Department.

"You got any murder warrants out?" he said to the lady who answered the phone.

"What is your name?"

Swindler answered, "He ain't got no name," and left the phone hanging by its cord.

Swindler figured he'd better get out of town, as well as get some money some way. He only knew one way.

He had already abandoned the Maverick and set out to find another car to steal.

Before long, he had stopped a university student, kidnapped him, and stolen his car. The college kid escaped when Swindler had to stop at a red light, and the student was able to open the passenger door. He ran like crazy to a phone booth to report the theft.

Knowing the police would soon be looking for him, Swindler abandoned the car when it ran out of gas and left it on a busy Columbia Street.

He found himself thinking about all the wrongs done to him in his life. He remembered his days of working at Edwards Nursery in Columbia. His boss had told Swindler that if he worked for cheap then, when he died, he'd leave the nursery and the little house Edwards lived in to Swindler. But the old man didn't leave a will, and Mrs. Edwards and her daughters refused to honor the verbal agreement. So, as an act of revenge, Swindler burned the little house down. That crime of arson was what led him to his first jail sentence and, as a consequence, the penchant for sex with men.

CHAPTER FIVE

Swindler started walking. There was bound to be a house close by where he could steal a car. He walked up to a dwelling that had been pretty at one time, but the shrubs around the house were overgrown and the sidewalk had wide cracks. The front door had a mail slot, and it and the porch furniture were stained by rust. It looked like old people lived there. He walked onto the porch and tapped on the brass door knocker. After a little while, an elderly woman opened the door.

"We're not buying anything."

Swindler pushed his way in. "You here alone?"

"No, my husband is upstairs asleep."

He looked around the kitchen. The cabinets were painted white and the counters were sparkling clean. No pans or dirty dishes or crumbs littered them. The floor was covered in linoleum that was designed to look like red bricks. Above the kitchen sink on a window ledge three African violets bloomed. A room air conditioner was attached to another window, but it wasn't working.

Swindler wiped the sweat from his brow with the tail of his shirt. "Man, it's hot in here. Your electric out or something?"

Even though it was the end of September, the days were still very warm. "We like to save money so we don't turn it on until late afternoon," she told the intruder.

Swindler thought she was a little huffy with her answer.

The husband came down to investigate an unfamiliar voice. He was a tall man with broad shoulders and a good-size belly. "Who the hell are you?" he asked.

"My name don't matter."

"What the hell you want?"

"I want your car and your money and them guns I seen in your gun cases."

The husband looked to his wife. She nodded her head yes, and put her hands together on her lap. "Do what he wants," she said.

It was clear to Swindler who wore the pants in the family.

He opened several kitchen drawers until he found a roll of masking tape which he used to tie up the couple.

"Where's your pocket book?" he asked the lady.

"Never mind," he said. "I see it now." He figured she kept the money that belonged to the family. He stole their Plymouth Duster that was parked in the garage, as well as the various guns he found in the gun cases. One was a beautiful rifle with a scope. The scope was still in the box.

After he left, they unwrapped their bindings and called the police. They later told detectives that the man did a lot of talking and acted like he wanted to be friendly, despite stealing their car and guns and what little money they had. The police figured their ages had probably saved their lives. Swindler's career had never involved the harming of the elderly. He was most interested in young men he could rape and torture. Old folks didn't cut it for him.

CHAPTER SIX

Swindler knew he needed to get out of South Carolina quickly so he got on an interstate which would take him west. In every other attempt to avoid capture he had stayed in the Southeast because he was most comfortable there.

After a couple of hours, he heard on the car's CB radio that the Plymouth Duster had been spotted by a Georgia state patrol car. Nervous that other cops were now looking for him, he stopped and parked behind an all-night gas station in Covington, Georgia. He could turn around and head for Florida. He liked Florida, especially Key West, where a lot of gay guys hung out in their tight Speedos. He wished he had a road map, but he laughed, wondering why, since he couldn't read it.

After a few hours of sleep, he left the car where he had parked it and walked to the front of the station. He asked for directions on the best way to get to Memphis. He then robbed the young attendant of the money in the cash register and locked him inside a closet. He tied up the man and told him not to attempt to get loose. While he was stealing some candy bars and chips, he heard the man in the closet grappling around, trying to get untied. He opened the door and shot the man in the back. The attendant was left bleeding on the floor, resulting in a long stay in the hospital, where doctors didn't know if the man would ever be able to walk again.

Swindler hadn't noticed a woman and her teenage son parked in front, witnessing what was happening. They called the police and gave the description of the man and the make of car he was driving, along with the license tag number.

Swindler left the station, still wondering if he should continue on west or turn around to head back down south to Florida. He flipped a coin, then two more. He pulled out at a fast pace, headed for his destination, Kansas City, where he had some grievances with a man he had met in prison.

He drove all night. When he got to the outskirts of Memphis, he picked up a hitchhiker, who told him how to get to a liquor store that opened early in the morning. Swindler sent the hitchhiker into the store for gin and a six pack of beer with a ten-dollar bill. He asked the hitchhiker if he knew how to get to Kansas City, and the man told him that if he'd drop him off where he lived, he'd give him a road map and mark the way he should go with a pen.

Swindler waited while the hitchhiker went into an old two-story house that had once seen glory days many years ago. A sign in the front read, *Rooms for Rent.*

The hitchhiker returned, panting. He said he lived on the second floor and had run up and down the stairs so quickly he was out of breath.

"You stay on 40 and then when you get to Alma, Arkansas, you take Highway 71 North. I'm going to circle it on this map."

Swindler thanked him and got back on the interstate. He would have robbed the guy, but he knew he didn't have any money or he wouldn't have been hitching.

After he had passed through Memphis, he stopped at a little store in West Memphis and bought some potted meat, bread, and mayonnaise. He'd already drunk all the six pack he'd bought earlier, but the store didn't sell beer.

In Forest City, Arkansas, he bought some more beer. The clerk told him he had a little more than an hour to travel to Little Rock. Swindler hoped to find J. D., a man he knew from prison, who owed him money.

CHAPTER SEVEN

The distance between Memphis and Little Rock takes about two hours and a few minutes but, to travelers, it seems like a lot longer. The road is flat, and the highway is paved in such a way that the tires make a thump, thump, thump sound that can soon drive you crazy. If you look out the window on either side of the road, there's nothing to see. Lots of big trucks travel the interstate. Most of the truck drivers know this is a stretch they can make up some time that they lost going through cities like Atlanta, Nashville, or Memphis.

Swindler pushed the Duster as hard as he could, even passing some of the trucks that were doing eighty or better.

When he reached the outskirts of Little Rock, he decided not to stop and look up J.D. He would do that on his way back home.

South Carolina was home, and he'd always return there.

Swindler looked at his map to follow the lines drawn on it by the hitchhiker. He saw Alma circled, and he remembered that was where he was supposed to turn north.

Because of the beer and gin, Swindler was feeling no pain by the time he made it to Alma. He zoomed by the exit which would have taken him north to Kansas City. By the time he realized he had missed the Alma turn, he was on a bridge crossing the Arkansas River.

Grumbling to himself for missing the highway to Kansas City, he exited at the first opportunity. He was almost blinded by the late September sun when he pulled in at a Road Runner Conoco Gas and Convenience Store on Kelley Highway. He decided he'd ask for directions. The Arkansas State Police building sat right across the street from the filling station, but Swindler never saw it because the sun was in his eyes.

CHAPTER EIGHT

Charles Lambert, or Chuck as he was known to family and friends, was a trooper with the Arkansas State Police. On September 24, he was working in the narcotics division and driving a yellow Volkswagen Beetle down Interstate 540. His destination was the Arkansas State Police Headquarters which was located on Kelley Highway and Interstate 540. It stood directly across the street from the Road Runner Conoco Gas and Convenience Store.

Trooper Lambert was dressed in blue jeans and a green and orange jungle-looking shirt. His hair was long and he wore a headband in the style of the people he normally arrested for drug activity. He was hoping to make a dent in the Fort Smith drug scene that night. He needed to pick up some instructions at the headquarters, so he parked at the back of the building and entered through a back door. He happened to look out the front window and saw a gold Plymouth Duster parked at the service station across the street. He had passed that car on the interstate and thought at the time that the driver looked like a suspicious character. The car had a South Carolina license plate.

"Look there, across the street. I seen that guy on the highway coming over here. I didn't like the way he looked."

Radio Operator Charles Vaughn shifted his gaze to where Chuck was pointing. He saw the gold Plymouth and a fat man walking toward the store entrance. "That may be the ugliest guy I've ever seen," he told Lambert. "No wonder you didn't like his looks."

Lambert went on about his business and filed the car away in the back of his mind.

CHAPTER NINE

Officer Basnett liked to stop at the Road Runner Station on Kelley Highway to have a Coke or coffee with Carl Tinder, who worked as an attendant in the convenience store at the gas station. Carl was a likable guy who only worked part-time at the station. His regular job was at Edwards Funeral Home. He and Basnett enjoyed each other and visited about sports at the University of Arkansas, only sixty or so miles north of Fort Smith. They both hoped the Razorbacks would have a good season in 1976. Both men were unsure if Frank Broyles was too old to coach. "This is Broyles' nineteenth season to coach. I guess he's going for twenty," said Basnett.

Frank Broyles was a legend in football. He had played at Georgia Tech, where he starred as the quarterback, before he became a coach and came to Arkansas in 1958. Tall and handsome, with a very strong Southern accent, he had won over the fans of Arkansas football. As long as his team was winning.

"He's got the best record money can buy," Tinder opined.

"You believe those stories about players getting paid under the table and new cars under their Christmas trees?"

"Say, Randy, how's the baby girl doing?"

"She's so great!"

"How old now? What? Three months?"

"She's three months and six days. She fell asleep on my stomach this morning while I was lying on our couch. She's so sweet."

Carl smiled, with just a pang of jealousy. He and his wife hadn't been able to have children. "Do you need to use the phone to call Cindy?"

"Thank you, Carl. But she and the kids have gone to my parents' house. Dad put up a swing set for Bill and Shannon."

Just then, a large, smelly man walked in and asked for help. "I can't read, and I need help getting to Alma. I drove right past it, and I was supposed to get off there on Highway 71 to get to Kansas City."

Mr. Tinder sighed, trying to think of the best way to tell a man who can't read how to get back on the right road. "Well, go back the way you came here on Kelley Highway, go over the interstate and turn left onto I-540 headed east, and then go over the river, and just past Van Buren, take the exit for I-40 to Little Rock. Then get off at Alma and take Highway 71 North to Kansas City."

Basnett dropped his empty Coke bottle in an almost empty Coke case by the side of the counter. "Well, good luck in Kansas City," he said to the man seeking directions. "I've got to get back to work."

Realizing that something seemed fishy, Carl Tinder watched Randy go to his car and pick up his radio and speak into it. He also saw the dirty guy who was lost leave and walk to his car. He raised the hood on his car and begin tinkering with something. Tinder felt a sense of relief that his buddy Basnett was close by. The smelly guy might have ideas of robbing the station.

Basnett had returned to his police car to check his clipboard for the information he and his fellow officers had received in the briefing before they started their shifts. They were to be on the lookout for a gold Plymouth Duster with South Carolina plates. He called headquarters and told them that the subject was at the Road Runner on Kelley Highway across from the State Police Headquarters. He asked that they be notified to help. He was advised to wait for backup, who were in the area and only minutes away.

Tinder saw Randy pull his police car around and park behind the Plymouth Duster. He watched Randy walk over and say something to the guy under the hood. He assumed Randy was asking for some identification.

Swindler looked up and Tinder heard him say, "Yeah, just a minute and I'll shut the hood. My license is in my car."

Randy waited for Swindler to get into his car to get his license out of his billfold. Randy walked closer and stood outside the driver's side window that was rolled down.

Swindler picked up the .38 caliber snub-nosed pistol that was lying on the seat beside him. In an instant he fired it point blank at Randy, hitting him twice, in the chest and abdomen.

Randy screamed in pain and got five or six shots off from his police-issued weapon as he was falling. He hit Swindler in his left thigh, the other bullets slamming into the side of the car.

Swindler started his car but the car stalled. He finally got it running and pulled out fast onto Kelley, screeching his tires as he fled.

At that moment, Chuck Lambert happened to look out the window toward the station again and witnessed the shoot-out. He grabbed his gun and ran out the front door. He fired off five shots as Swindler drove by in the Plymouth Duster.

Because Swindler was not familiar with the area, he drove down the north end of Kelley and came to a dirt road that led down to a soybean field planted on the banks of the Arkansas River.

Chuck saw where he went and got into his little Volkswagen to begin pursuit. Officer Bob Ross arrived on the scene, and Chuck waved him down and told him the route Swindler took. Ross told Chuck to get out of his little yellow Volkswagen and go with him.

Ross's patrol unit stalled. "Shit, ain't this the luck." He cranked it again, but still the motor whined.

Lambert let out a string of cuss words.

"We'll take Randy's unit," Ross yelled. They then ran back to Randy's police car, climbed in, but it, too, stalled. Finally, Ross got it running and they took off.

Randy was still lying on the pavement, and Carl Tinder had already called an ambulance. He stayed with Randy, but he thought his friend had probably already died. The ambulance had arrived as Officer Ross and Chuck Lambert left.

Carl Tinder later said, "I'd been in the funeral business a long time. I could see that his eyes were fixed and that he would soon be gone."

Customers Steven Cardwell and his wife pulled into the convenience store about the time the shoot-out was gearing up. Cardwell had gone inside the store to buy a few things for the weekend while his wife stayed in the car.

She was safely inside, but she witnessed and heard all the shooting, and she was afraid her husband was going to get caught in the middle of it.

By the time Cardwell rushed safely back to their car, his wife was sobbing and screaming. He took her to their nearby home but, not wanting to miss anything, he returned to the scene.

Plymouth Duster abandoned in brush in Arkansas River bottoms.

Plymouth Duster with bullet holes from Basnett's gun fired
after Swindler shot him in the stomach two times

CHAPTER TEN

A deeply wooded area bordered the Arkansas River, and Swindler pulled his car into the vine-snarled woods. Bob Ross knew there was a small fishing camp close to the river. He and Chuck got out of their car and started fanning out toward that area. Soon they were joined by three other officers who'd arrived shortly after the shooting.

They saw the gold Plymouth Duster bottomed out in big heavy undergrowth. The driver's side door was opened. Then they heard shouting. It was Swindler.

"I'm giving myself up. I don't want to be killed."

The lawmen cautiously moved toward the yelling, afraid there might be an ambush. The heavy undergrowth and trees kept it almost impossible to see Swindler. Finally, after moving toward the sound very slowly, they saw him, with his arms held high. They told him to lean against a tree and stay there. They then moved in and handcuffed him and marched him to a police car. Being none too gentle, they practically threw him into the back seat.

"You better hope you didn't kill Randy," one of the officers yelled at Swindler.

In the immediate area where Swindler had surrendered, they found a high-powered rifle with a scope, two .38 caliber revolvers, and one .22 semi-automatic pistol. All the guns were loaded.

CHAPTER ELEVEN

Randy Basnett died in the ambulance on the way to Sparks Hospital. He had been a brave officer, performing his duty as he had sworn to do.

Two months before, when he was asleep following a long shift, he was awakened by a phone call. The Fort Smith Police were requesting all off-duty policemen to report for duty. A well-respected police officer had been shot in the head, and there was an APB out for the person who had shot him. Randy had jumped up and in moments had his uniform on. He had finished strapping his gun on when he kissed Cindy and headed for the door.

Cindy had called him back. "Randy, I love you. I want you to promise me that you will be careful. I love you so much. What would we do without you?"

Randy had paused and taken Cindy in his arms. He kissed her. "I promise I'll be careful."

Later, in the early morning hours he called Cindy. "I'm sorry to wake you, honey, but I want you to know I'm okay. I'll be home as soon as I finish this paperwork."

But on this night, he wasn't able to call his wife.

Dr. Kent Smith, a Fort Smith pathologist, performed the autopsy on Randy Basnett. As an Assistant Medical Examiner for the State of Arkansas, he was qualified to perform the autopsy of a person who died under suspicious circumstances. Several police officers were there to watch.

Doctor Kent Smith was a handsome, gentle man with brown curly hair. He was used to having an audience of policemen while he performed his examinations.

Dr. Smith cautioned the men. "Because I'll be performing this autopsy on one of you, I want you to search your hearts and stomachs to see if you can stay and watch."

He looked around the room and smiled before his face grew stern. He said, "This brave hero may have been a special friend to you, so if you want to leave, now's the time. I don't want to be disturbed by people leaving the room."

When Dr. Smith saw that nobody was leaving, he began the work he'd trained years to do. His results concluded that Basnett died of one bullet that penetrated the abdomen, lacerated the intestines, and sliced the aorta, all of which caused massive bleeding. The doctor retrieved the bullet from under the skin on the back of his chest.

The second bullet would have caused paralysis in the legs and feet because of the laceration of the spinal cord. Dr. Smith retrieved the bullet that was lodged in the cord. The second bullet also caused massive bleeding. The official cause of death was from sudden blood loss. Either wound would have killed him.

The good doctor gave the .38 bullets to Detective Bob Hatfield who had watched the autopsy. The detective then turned the bullets in to the evidence custodian. It was later determined that the bullets came from Swindler's revolver.

When Dr. Smith finished and wrote up his findings, he wondered if there was still light enough for him to go home and work in his yard. He loved gardening, and his two-story pale-yellow house located in Hillcrest, a charming old section of Fort Smith, was beautifully set in a blanket of green grass. Soon the maple trees with orange and yellow leaves would cast a lovely golden shadow on his house he shared with his pretty blonde wife, Ann.

He needed beauty in his life, especially right now.

CHAPTER TWELVE

Detective Hatfield would have liked to escape the remembrances of the autopsy. But he had another chore: gathering the bloody police shirt Basnett had worn when he was killed.

Another detective, Charles Jankowski, had also witnessed the autopsy. He was in charge of the clothes Swindler had worn when arrested: two articles of clothing, a pair of khaki pants, and shoes. In Swindler's front pockets were a billfold holding a security card, a rent receipt, a two-dollar bill, and twenty-four cents in change. Swindler also carried a small screwdriver and several rounds of .38 Special ammunition.

Across the hall from the morgue and down a way was treatment room 7, where Dr. Harley Darnall, an emergency room physician, was treating John Edward Swindler. His smelly clothes had been removed for evidence, and he was clad in a white prison uniform that had previously been worn by another extremely large prisoner. It smelled like all prison uniforms smelled, reeking of laundry detergent and bleach.

Swindler had a swollen face with a busted lip that he claimed had come after he was captured and beaten by officers with shotguns.

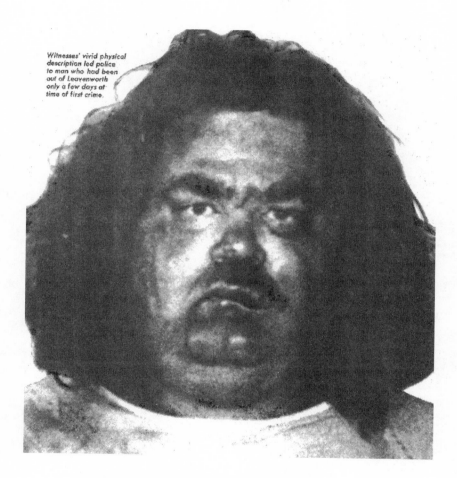

Witnesses' vivid physical description led police to man who had been out of Leavenworth only a few days at time of first crime.

Swindler after he was arrested and brought to hospital.

Dr. Darnall disputed Swindler's later claim that he had been beaten with the butt end of a shotgun. Dr. Darnall testified in court that his jaw would have been broken and his teeth would have been knocked out. As it was, forty small stitches had been taken in his face. A rumor circulated in the hospital that the doctors who treated Swindler used no pain medicine.

Swindler's wound in his left thigh, inflicted in the last seconds of Officer Basnett's life, was also treated in the emergency room.

After being mortally wounded by two shots from Swindler's revolver, Basnett had fallen and then raised up and fired all six bullets from his weapon at Swindler while the murderer was still sitting in his car.

When Basnett died, his gun was still in his hand. And Swindler had a bullet in his left thigh.

CHAPTER THIRTEEN

As Randy Basnett was taking his last breath, Cindy was changing their daughter's diaper. Randy's mother stood over Cindy and watched Cindy's fingers effortlessly remove the soiled diaper and quickly pin another one around the baby's bottom.

"Oh, she's so adorable," Peggy Basnett said. "I think she looks just like her daddy."

Cindy chuckled. "Randy thinks so too, but my daddy thinks she's the spitting image of me."

"Oh, I'm not surprised at that. Your daddy thinks the sun rose and set with you. It's so funny to see the way he dotes on his little girl."

"Mama spoils me just as much."

Peggy raised her head and held her finger to her lips. "Shh, I just heard something on the scanner."

The police scanner was a gift to Peggy Basnett from her son. He told her to keep it on the kitchen cabinet and she could keep track of him. Randy thought his mother was a born worrier, and the scanner would allay her fears.

Both women listened to the scanner: There had been shots fired on the north side of town at the corner of Kelley Highway and I-540.

"That's Randy's beat!" Cindy yelled. She quickly calmed her voice. She didn't want to alarm everybody. She walked to the window over the sink and looked out. Bill and Shannon were having a blast, swinging on the new swing set Randy's dad had bought for them. Trying not to alarm Peggy any more than she was, Cindy said, "My kids sure do like their swing set."

Peggy whispered, "Go to the back bedroom and call the police department and ask what's going on."

Cindy did as Peggy asked and shut the bedroom door behind her. She dialed the number and finally got an answer from the dispatcher. He wouldn't tell her anything. "Mrs. Basnett, I'm not allowed to divulge any details. Just tell me where you are? Home?"

"No, I'm at my in-laws, Randy's folks. His mother heard something on the scanner that has scared us. Please, I've got to know something."

The dispatcher hesitated before answering. "Mrs. Basnett, we'll notify you as soon as we know anything."

Cindy hung up the phone. She felt like turning back the chenille bedspread and crawling under the sheets. Instead, she walked back into the kitchen to tell her mother-in-law that she couldn't find out anything.

Cindy needed her parents, but she knew they had plans to go fishing at Tenkiller with friends and spend the weekend there. She was relieved when the friends who were going with her parents walked in the back patio with a loud "Hello, how's everybody?"

Cindy let out a long sigh of relief, knowing that her parents were still home. She went back into the bedroom and this time called her parents. Her daddy answered the phone and she started crying.

"We've heard the news about the shooting, honey."

"I'm here at Randy's parents. Can you come over? Amanda's asleep and Bill and Shannon are in the backyard having fun."

"We'll be right there, darling."

Cindy and her daddy sat down in the living room, waiting for someone to come and notify them of something. Either Randy was dead, or badly injured. The knock on the door came, and her daddy opened it.

Ben Stephens stood there with his head lowered. He was the chaplain with the Fort Smith Police Department, and it was his unfortunate duty to first speak to the families.

Cindy stood close to Stephens, and hit him on his chest over and over again. "Don't tell me Randy's dead. Don't you dare come here and tell me that."

Her father, as a former policeman, knew that survivors of brutal murders committed on loved ones reacted differently to the news. Some would lash out at the messenger. Others might be gracious and profusely thankful for the personal visit instead of an impersonal phone call. Some might forever associate the messenger with the memory of the death of their loved one.

In this case, Cindy Basnett and Ben Stephens later became devoted friends. Cindy recognized Stephens as a true Christian who helped her heal and, from the first pounding fist to an eventual lasting friendship, Cindy experienced a calmness upon clasping Stephens' hands whenever or wherever she might find him.

Stephens explained that Randy's body was at Sparks Hospital and that his family could see him after an autopsy was conducted.

"Why an autopsy? We know a man shot him twice in the stomach."

"It's routine, daughter."

Cindy wiped her cheeks with her fingers. "Let's go now."

"We have to wait until they tell us we can come."

"But Daddy, I want to see him now!"

"Cynthia."

She knew that when her daddy called her Cynthia, he meant business. "Okay, Daddy. I'm sorry, but I'm so sad. And so mad."

Cindy's doctor called the senior Basnett home on Iona Street, identified himself as her doctor, and asked if her mom or dad was there. Peggy Basnett called Mr. Davis to the phone. He then told her dad that Cindy probably needed a sedative, and he should take her to St. Edward Hospital. He was going to call the emergency room, and they'd be expecting her.

Cindy and her daddy left the Basnett home and drove straight to the new St. Edward Hospital that had been open only eleven months. They were lucky and parked in a space close to the emergency entrance. The September day was almost gone, and a dusky evening was settling in. The pavement was hot to Cindy's feet which were still clad in her sandals she had pulled on early that morning.

She reached for her daddy's hand. He squeezed it so hard, she had to say, "Daddy, you're hurting me."

"Oops, sorry."

"My rings were rubbing together. That's what was wrong."

Her daddy held the door for her when they entered the ER. The waiting area was full of people, as it usually was on Friday night. Her daddy recognized a man sitting by himself in the corner by some windows. Her daddy nodded and said hello, and the man nodded as well. He looked very sad and Cindy wondered what was wrong in his life. That's when she realized that everyone had tragedy in their lives, and this was hers and Randy's.

They stopped at a window staffed by an older woman with dyed black hair. She smiled and asked if she could help them.

"We were told by Dr. Tom Whitaker to come here to the ER for a shot, a sedative, I guess. He is my daughter's doctor. Her name is Cindy Basnett."

"Yes, I have the order right here. I'll get a nurse right quick. Just take a seat, and I'll call you."

Cindy and her daddy had barely sat down for a minute when they were called back. A pleasant-looking nurse with blonde hair took them back to a room that had a gurney off to the side of the room. There were windows on one side. It didn't look like an emergency room. It looked more like a conference room.

"Mrs. Basnett, we wanted to give you some privacy. If you'll just lie down on this gurney, I'll be right back with Dr. Whitaker's orders."

"I can't believe how nice everyone is," Cindy said as she lay down. "Did you call the doctor?"

"No, honey. He called us and told me to bring you here for something to help you deal with all this."

Tears welled up in Cindy's blue eyes. "That's so nice of him."

The nurse came back in with a tray that contained a vial of medicine and a needle. "You want this in your hip? You don't have much meat back there, do you? Let me try your arm. I've been giving injections for twenty-five years. I won't hurt you."

It did hurt Cindy, but she didn't want to say so.

Her daddy had been standing by the gurney, holding her hand. "Well, when you feel like it, we'll go home. Your mom has the kids there with her. We need to feed you."

They stayed for five minutes or so until Cindy announced she was ready to go home. "I want to see my kids, Daddy. I don't want them to think they've lost me too."

CHAPTER FOURTEEN

In Muldrow, Oklahoma, a man was watching Channel 5 News. He was tired from mowing the yard and weeding his small garden that was coming right along. He had more tomatoes than he could give away, a bumper okra crop, and bell peppers so green and shiny that, combined with the tomatoes, it looked like a Christmas garden.

He'd finished two tall glasses of lemonade, put up his feet in his recliner, and heard the newscaster give a special report that a Fort Smith policeman was killed in a shoot-out at a convenience store/gas station on Kelly Highway in north Fort Smith.

A picture of his grandson, Randy Basnett, appeared on the screen. "Oh, my God!" Deke Fant shouted out.

His wife came running out of the kitchen with a dishtowel thrown over her shoulder. "What is it?"

"I just heard on the TV that Randy's been shot. They took the guy who did it to Sparks Hospital."

Deke looked at the woman who was his second wife, the lady he married after Randy's grandmother died. "Some guy wanted out of South Carolina shot Randy and killed him over at that place on Kelly Highway.

The service station that's across the street from the Arkansas State Police headquarters. It's the one I like to stop at for my Redman."

"We better call your daughter. They may need us."

"You do it. I've got something to do."

His wife saw the veins in his forehead pop out, and his face exploded a beet red. "What you got to do?" she asked.

He didn't answer her. He was headed down the hall to the closet where he kept his shotgun. "Don't try to stop me," he yelled. "I just told you. I've got something I've got to do."

Without another word spoken, Deke grabbed a handful of shells and dropped them in his front pants pocket. He opened the kitchen door that led to the garage. He reached for the door handle on his truck, and stood for a moment. He then went back to the kitchen door and hollered to his wife. "Don't tell Randy's mom, but I'm going to the hospital and finish the job Randy started."

Deke pulled out on Hwy 64, which would take him across the Arkansas River Bridge out of Oklahoma and into Arkansas. He ran into the usual Friday night traffic that was brought on by high school football events. There were two high schools in Fort Smith, but only one stadium, and it was behind Northside High School on Rogers Avenue. He needed to get on Towson to go to Sparks.

He was careful with his speed, knowing that the police patrolled the streets heavily on game nights, so he made sure he followed the speed limits down to Sparks Hospital.

When Deke pulled into the parking lot, he saw three police cars parked at the emergency entrance. Beige uniforms were clustered at the door. He realized, at that moment, that he could not get inside the hospital with his shotgun. Not with all those police outside. He decided to leave his shotgun on the floorboard. He locked the doors and walked over to the men.

Before he realized it, he felt his eyes fill with tears and his voice shook like he was scared. "Guys, I'm Randy's grandpa."

The policemen grew quiet. They all looked down at the pavement. Not knowing what to say.

One of the men had met Randy's grandpa at a family picnic that the city of Fort Smith put on for the police department. Deke had been Randy's honored guest.

"Hi there, Deke. I'm Marvin Gates. I met you a few years ago at a police picnic. Randy introduced us."

"Yes, I remember, Marvin. That was a real nice day. Not like this one here."

CHAPTER FIFTEEN

Cindy was asleep in her parents' bedroom. The shot she got at the hospital had relaxed her enough that she was able to go to sleep and sleep soundly. The phone was constantly ringing from people who had heard the bad news. Most were good friends, but some were mere acquaintances. And the food was piling up from friends who didn't know what else to do but bring a pie or a casserole or sandwich makings.

The doorbell rang and Cindy's daddy went to the door. The two men standing outside, wearing dark suits, identified themselves as FBI agents

"I'm Odell Davis," he said, holding his hand out to each one and shaking it.

The taller man offered his condolences and explained why they were there. "We were told we could find Mrs. Basnett here."

"Yes, I'm her father." He pointed to the brown living room couch. "You fellas want to sit down?"

"We came to see your daughter, sir."

Cindy's daddy looked at his watch. He realized that his only child, his precious daughter, had been asleep for four hours, which was a long nap. "I'll get her for you."

Cindy awoke at her daddy's touch. "What is it now?" she asked.

"Some FBI agents are here and want to talk to you. They won't be long, I'm sure. I'll see to it."

"Let me go to the bathroom and comb my hair and wash my face."

Her daddy walked back into the living room. "She's coming, but don't be too long, guys. She has been through hell and back."

The men rose from their seats when Cindy came in the room. "We wanted to tell you that John Swindler was not paroled. He was given a release from prison in Leavenworth, Kansas, by the warden, Charles Benson, because he caused so much trouble that the warden couldn't control him even by placing him in solitary confinement. So, Swindler should not have been out, and as a result of the warden's weakness, Swindler has killed three people and wounded several more.

Cindy put her hand to her mouth. She looked at her daddy who was standing next to her. Her shoulders began to shake before she started crying. She didn't cry long. And after wiping away her tears on a handkerchief her daddy handed her, she said, "Well, I want that warden fired!"

"Yes, ma'am. We do too," the tall one said.

The other agent said, "When we heard about this, we decided you needed to know."

Cindy put her shoulders back. She wasn't crying anymore. She was too mad to cry. "Let me know when that SOB is fired, will you?"

In unison, the men said, "Yes, ma'am."

CHAPTER SIXTEEN

The handsome brave policeman, loving husband, and father was the first Fort Smith officer killed in the line of duty since 1938.

The bravery of Randy Basnett was talked about in every beauty salon and barber shop, every coffee shop and restaurant, every home in a hundred-mile area. On future Sunday mornings, preachers spoke from the pulpit on nobility and bravery of our policemen.

It was only days later that those same people who had spoken so highly of the brave policeman who was shot down were talking about Swindler with a bad taste in their mouths.

They found out that Swindler was wanted for the murders of two teenagers in South Carolina, numerous kidnappings and car thefts, and that he was a homosexual who had asked newsmen if there was a Gay Rights office in Fort Smith. In 1976, some folks thought his sexual preference was as sinful as murder.

And when his pictures appeared on television and in the newspapers, he looked like a savage bear, with his wild red hair and huge jowls and big lips. Then folks learned he had been judged competent to stand trial by the doctors at the State Hospital in Little Rock.

"Why, you can tell he's crazy just by looking at him," voiced more than one husband to his wife over coffee at breakfast.

CHAPTER SEVENTEEN

Finally, they decided on one. The next choice, which turned out to be harder, was to pick where to have the service.

"Cynthia, I've been talking to Randy's good friends, and they say lots of people will be attending the service."

"Where are you suggesting, Daddy?"

"At the Civic Center."

"No! Hell, no! That's where events are held. I don't want his funeral to be an event. No way is that going to happen."

"Just think about it. Your Baptist church in Barling is too small. The First Baptist Church of Fort Smith has offered, but their minister is not sure even the church sanctuary there is large enough."

Cindy's daddy knew his daughter was a "pistol" and always stood up for what she believed. He could see that she would handle this tragedy with the strength she received from her Savior.

"Tomorrow we'll go down to Edwards Funeral Home for the viewing. You can see Randy for the first time. And last time."

Cindy held her daddy's hand while they prepared to enter the front door of Edwards Funeral Home. The Presbyterian Church across the street from the funeral home was having a funeral, and the parking lot used by both was busy with people getting out of their cars.

Delmer Edwards met them when they walked in. He spoke warmly and offered his condolences once again. He led them into the room where Randy lay, dressed in his police uniform. Two policemen stood by his side.

Cindy began to sob, and she asked her daddy if he would ask the policemen to leave. "I want to be alone with Randy."

Cindy leaned over the casket and told him over and over again that she loved him. "You've been the best husband and the best father. Thank you for loving Shannon and Bill. And Amanda will never get to go fishing with you. I am so mad that you got killed by that horrible guy. I hate him, I hate him, I hate him!"

Cindy's daddy eased her away because she was getting close to acting hysterical. He began to talk to Randy by saying, "I love you, son. We sure had a lot of fun fishing together." He then patted Randy's chest with his hand and said, "I'm going to see that you get justice, son. I'm going to see to it if it's the last thing I do."

They stood by the casket for ten or fifteen minutes. Cindy whispered to her daddy, "I don't want to leave him. He's all alone, Daddy."

The policemen were standing outside the door when they left. Cindy thanked them and her daddy shook their hands. "Thank you for honoring him," he told the men whose eyes were glistening with tears. "Thank you from our entire family."

CHAPTER EIGHTEEN

Cindy reluctantly agreed that the service could be held at the Fort Smith Civic Center. She didn't want to have her husband there for a show, she said. But Randy's parents agreed with her daddy. And her mother convinced her that there were a lot of people who wanted to come and pay their respects to the hero who took out Swindler. Officers from all around would be coming to pay their respects to another officer killed in the line of duty.

Even Randy's fourth-grade teacher, Mrs. DeWitt, attended the funeral service and signed the guest book.

Services were held in late September at the Civic Center, and it was filled with people. When Cindy looked around and saw the full house, she once again felt like she was at an event instead of her husband's funeral. She was seated on the first row, and the casket was at the middle of the stage on a riser. It was draped with an American flag which was later ceremoniously folded and given to her.

Two ministers spoke, along with Ben Stephens, the police chaplain who had first told Cindy that her husband was dead. When words of comfort were mercifully over, the family made the procession by the casket.

Cindy was sobbing, and when she kissed the casket, she wanted to stay with him and finish the conversation she had started with him the moment she found out he was dead. Among the many things she wanted to tell him was that her parents had sold their house.

Randy Basnett's body on view at funeral held in Fort Smith's Municipal Auditorium.

At last, she and her family left the Civic Center and began the drive to Roselawn Cemetery.

Suddenly Cindy screamed, "Stop the car!"

The passengers stopped their conversations, and the only sounds were the tires screeching on the concrete streets, Cindy once again yelled out that she wanted the car to stop.

The driver pulled the family car to the side of the road. "I wasn't through talking with Randy. While there's time, take me back to him right now," Cindy explained to her mother who sat next to her. Both women were crying.

The driver looked at Cindy's father for instruction. He nodded his head yes, and the driver turned the car around and headed back to the Civic Center.

The coffin containing Randy was still on the stage. The funeral home employees were loading up the many floral arrangements to take to the cemetery when Cindy and her daddy returned. Cindy's daddy explained that his daughter wanted to be with her husband for a little while.

Cindy was able to talk to her husband about their little girl, Amanda. She also promised her husband she'd be brave and make him proud of her.

None of the bystanders were able to keep tears from falling.

Cindy Basnett accepts the American flag honoring her husband.

Long procession of cars on route to Roselawn Cemetery.

Cindy Basnett bids farewell to her husband.

CHAPTER NINETEEN

Cindy worked hard to establish a routine to get through each day. She packed each hour full of her caretaking responsibilities. The baby, Amanda, required the most attention, of course. All the children sensed the sadness of their mother and the frightening disappearance of their father from their daily lives. They heard about the murder of their father on television, often interrupting their Saturday morning cartoons.

In the meantime, Swindler was up to frighteningly dirty tricks. Other prisoners were afraid of him, and only a fool wouldn't be. He convinced one of his fellow inmates to see that his girlfriend, who worked the prison's emergency switchboard, would make late night phone calls to Cindy's house. When Cindy answered, a recording would say "Wait for an emergency phone call." Of course, her first thoughts were that her parents were injured in a car wreck or that Randy's mother and dad were hurt. Cindy knew all too well that when a tragedy happens in your life, you know that it can happen again because it's already happened once to you, you're always prepared for the worst.

When Cindy was in her car, nearly always with her three children, she would look in the rearview mirror and notice that a car was following her with menacing-looking men inside. This happened many times and she always notified the police, who kept a watch on her home in Barling. She got an unlisted telephone number, but that didn't help. She continued to get the calls, always late at night. The police finally found out about the girlfriend at the jail switchboard and fired her.

CHAPTER TWENTY

Carl and Ruth Tinder lived on South 26th Street, an historical area of Fort Smith that still had brick streets. Next door lived Police Major Paul Rivaldo with his wife and three children.

The Tinders were "salt of the earth" folks. Carl worked for Edwards Funeral Home and had a part-time job at the convenience store/gas station on Kelley Highway where he had witnessed the death of his friend, Randy Basnett. Carl would be a witness at the coming trial of Swindler.

Carl was relaxing in his pretty living room, decorated in the Victorian style by his wife, Ruth, when the phone rang. Carl answered and a threatening voice shouted out, "You're a dead man if you testify."

Tinder was so shocked that he didn't know how to reply to the threat. "Who the hell are you?" he asked

They had already been getting hang-up phone calls late at night. They notified the police who thought it might be coming from Swindler and his cronies, whom he'd intimidated to do his dirty work.

A police unit was assigned to watch the Tinder home as well as Rivaldo's home. The Rivaldos had reported phone calls from someone with a very Southern-sounding drawl, always asking the question, "Is this the cop's house?" And then hanging up.

The police took the threatening phone calls seriously. They assigned officers to stay with the Tinders at night, guarding them and keeping watch over the Rivaldo home as well. Ruth Tinder made a big pot of coffee each night for the officers to have during their stay. And sometimes she stopped at Von Hatten's Bakery, which was on her way home from work, and pick up various pastries for the officers to have with their coffee.

The Tinder's bedroom was at the back of the house. When they went to bed they closed their bedroom door each night. This arrangement lasted for a few weeks. The policemen had rigged up some sort of trap laid out in the yard on either side of the house. It was composed of dry twigs, piles of leaves, and plastic objects which would make noise if stepped upon.

On the third week, the policemen heard something and looked out a darkened window and saw two men in the back yard. They knew no men should be there at one o'clock in the morning.

The policemen tiptoed into the Tinder's bedroom and woke them.

One whispered in a gravely smoker's voice, "Don't turn on the light. We want you to get out of bed and come with us into the living room."

Ruth was trying to get fully awake. Her husband was still asleep.

"Carl, Carl," she whispered as loudly as she dared. She poked on his shoulder. "The police have heard something."

The men knew that the lamp was on Carl's bedside table. "Don't turn on the light, Carl."

Ruth was already out of bed, pulling on her robe.

"Carl, are you awake?" one of the men asked.

"I am now."

"We saw someone in your back yard. We want you to come into the living room and sit with us until morning."

Tinder home guarded by police.

Ruth and Carl had no children, and the couple was used to nice, quiet evenings at home. The policemen were concerned that Ruth would be so frightened she might scream out. She had surprised them. Carl seemed to be the one most upset. He had a few profane words to say about not wanting his wife frightened.

CHAPTER TWENTY-ONE

Next door, Major Rivaldo and his wife, Mary, were discussing the events of the night before at the Tinder's house. There were two pretty teenage girls in the family, and they knew their girls would be especially inviting to the scumbags who did Swindler's bidding. Their son was a good-looking Italian boy who favored his father, but just because he was a male didn't mean he wouldn't be assaulted.

After her husband left for work, her three children were eating breakfast. Mary said, "I've talked to Geraldine, and she said you kids and I could stay at her house for as long as we need."

"Why? Is it what happened next door?" asked Kathy, the oldest of the children, and the most inquisitive.

"Your dad and I want to keep you safe. It's just being cautious. And since we both work …"

The neighborhood kids knew trouble was happening at the Tinder house. To the kids, the police stakeout was exciting news.

The next day, Mary Rivaldo took her children to her best friend's house. Her husband, Paul, would be staying in their son's room. Each child took enough clothes to last a week. When the week was over, Mary took them home. When the weekend was over, Mary and the kids went back to Geraldine's for the next week.

Kathy, the oldest and the nosiest, went to Northside High School, which was close to her home on 26th Street. One day early in their hideout phase of life, she realized that she needed her pearl earrings and necklace to wear for the class picture. On the noon hour, instead of eating lunch at school, she ran home to get her pearls. The front door key was under a blue ceramic flower pot. She let herself in and checked to see what was in the fridge, but found nothing she liked. Careful to not make a mess in the kitchen, she fixed a peanut butter sandwich. She then ran up the stairs to the bedroom she shared with her sister. Her parents' bedroom door was closed, which was unusual, so Kathy opened the door. What she saw was frightening! Guns were lying on the bed. Lots of them. Some black stocking caps and black shirts and pants were stacked in a chair. The bed had been moved closer to the window that looked down on the Tinder's house. Kathy quickly grasped the seriousness of their mother taking them out of their home. Here on the bed was proof that there was real danger in their lives.

Kathy was a popular, spunky girl who always prided herself on her bravery. She was short and had the "nobody better take advantage of me" personality that seems to be a trait of some short people. But on that day, her bravery disappeared as she ran down the stairs into the kitchen. She left by way of the front door and ran across the street before she realized she hadn't left the key under the front flower pot. She had to go back and raced across the street, tucking the key under the pot. This time she ran toward school on the sidewalk where the Tinder's front steps were. "Oh Lord, please don't let those men get me," she prayed all the way back to school. She couldn't wait to tell her sister and brother what she'd seen.

"But don't tell Mom and Dad."

Later, Kathy found out that the police had used her parents' bedroom to keep watch over the Tinder's house. The clothes were there in case the policemen needed to put them on and sneak over to the Tinder's house and arrest whoever was stalking around there. Even though the Tinder family was in hiding, chances were that the Swindler thugs did not know that. The guns were there in case of an emergency that would have to be dealt with quickly. The bedroom window could be raised and guns fired from that point. Suddenly, the reality of what had been exciting to Kathy took a deadly serious turn.

CHAPTER TWENTY-TWO

Ruth and Carl Tinder weren't happy about the police department's decision to move them to a safe location. "No damn crazy man is going to run me out of my home," Carl said.

He was overruled by Ruth and the prosecuting attorney's office. They didn't want anybody messing with their case and the chance to put Swindler away for good.

They were settled in at a Holiday Inn motel on 10th and B. It wasn't far from Ruth's employment at Weldon, Williams, and Wick. Or Carl's job at Edwards Funeral Home.

Ruth was at work, sitting at her desk, when the phone rang. She answered and a voice on the other end said, "Your husband's a dead man."

Ruth slammed the phone down in its cradle. Her heart was jumping and she felt faint. She had a Coke on her desk she'd been nursing along, and she picked it up and downed it quickly.

The phone rang again, and Ruth let it ring six or seven times before she picked it up. She hesitantly answered, "Hello?"

"You're a dead woman."

Before she even called her husband, she called their neighbor Paul Rivaldo at the police station.

She was told to wait a minute for Rivaldo because he was working in the radio room. After several minutes Major Rivaldo came to the phone. "Ruth, what can I do for you?"

"Oh, Paul, I've just gotten a phone call here at work. The voice was real Southern sounding. And mean sounding. He threatened to kill me if Carl testified."

"Now, Ruth, we'll take care of this. What time are you off this afternoon?"

"At five, but I don't know how I can stay here that long. I'm pretty shook up."

"Well, I'll come get you right now. You tell your boss what has happened, and I'll meet you at the front door in fifteen minutes."

"Bless you for taking care of us."

"Ruth, it's the Fort Smith Police Department doing what's right. We'll watch over you and Carl. I wonder how Swindler knew where you worked."

Major Rivaldo hung up the phone, shook his head in disbelief, and uttered some cuss words that he wouldn't want his wife, Mary, to hear. Mary was a beautiful woman. Everybody said so, and his buddies at the station teased him about how an "I-talian" like him grabbed hold of her.

Rivaldo went into the Men's Room to check his appearance. He'd been working on some equipment that was dirty and full of black ink that had cemented into a hard piece of rubber. He washed his hands and combed his thick, black hair, adjusted the tie at his collar, and hummed a tune in order to calm himself. The Tinders were a great couple, and he hated that the bastard Swindler had the moxie to scare some good folks who tried hard to be good citizens of their community.

It took five minutes for Rivaldo to get to Ruth's place of employment. Weldon, Williams, and Lick employed good people and always treated their employees fairly. Nobody ever quit their job because they knew how lucky they were to work where they did.

Ruth was standing behind the glass door that led into the offices. She raised her hand in a wave when she saw him. Her lips were trembling a little, and she was fighting back tears.

Rivaldo hopped out of the driver's side of his police car, and opened the passenger side door for Ruth. "I'm so sorry your and Carl's lives have been interrupted by Swindler."

"When do you think the trial will officially start?"

"Well, they are starting pre-trial conferences now. Judge Holland is anxious to get this trial going. He doesn't want to move it out of Sebastian County. It would be too expensive, for one thing, and difficult for traveling to court."

Ruth sighed. "The hotel is nice, and the food is good. I just miss my bed and puttering around my house. Carl misses his hobbies. He likes antique cars, you know?"

"Ruth, this Swindler guy is a horrible man. He reminds me of that savage Indian in that movie … oh, what's its name? John Wayne was in it."

"You must mean Scar in "The Searchers.""

"Yes, that's the one. So you remember the Indian I'm talking about?"

"Yeah, but I hid my eyes in those scary parts." Ruth ducked her head and chuckled. "Although, I always had my eyes on John Wayne."

By the time they reached the motel, Ruth and Paul had discussed lots of movies they both liked: "The Godfather," "Cool Hand Luke," and "Benji," which they both agreed was a sweet story.

Carl was waiting for Ruth at the motel's elevators. He shook hands with his neighbor and major in the police department. "Thanks for bringing her here. I sure hope we don't have to put up with this much longer. You know, I've never seen a human being more threatening than Swindler. Or frightening."

CHAPTER TWENTY-THREE

At long last, the trial was scheduled to begin. Swindler's attorneys asked that the charge of capital felony murder against Swindler be reduced to first degree murder. The presiding judge, John Holland, denied that request

Swindler's attorneys also asked for a change in venue because of all the negative publicity in Sebastian County. Judge Holland denied that motion.

On a cold February day in 1977, ninety-six potential jurors showed up at Sebastian County Courthouse. The defendant appeared in a yellow shirt and brown pants. His hair was still long, but it had obviously been shampooed and trimmed.

It was evident that the courtroom was heavily guarded. Deputies, clad in green blazers, were seated in the courtroom. Some had walkie-talkies. Attendees had been scanned for weapons with a metal detector, a new device never used before by the county.

The primary question asked of the first twenty-four prospective jurors by Attorney Charles Karr was, "Do you believe in the death penalty?" If the person answered "No," then the judge dismissed him or her. If a person answered, "Yes," then he or she was asked if, when it came right down to it, they could really impose the death penalty on the defendant. That question proved to the hardest to answer truthfully.

Those who said they believed in the death penalty were asked to remain in the courthouse.

Next came the selection of the jury which is a process called voir dire, which in Latin means "to tell the truth." Each side questions potential jurors about their backgrounds and any prior knowledge about the murder trial. Each side can dismiss someone "for cause" if they detect a person may be biased in a way that would cause them to favor either the prosecution or the defense.

By three o'clock that afternoon, Judge Holland approved a panel of six men and six women: two Fort Smith school teachers, five housewives, a retired railroad worker, chief maintenance at Arkansas Air National Guard, owner of a mobile home company, a home construction firm president, and a church building superintendent. Two men were chosen as alternates.

At the end of the day, Swindler asked reporters if there were any Gay Liberation Society meetings in the area. He said he was denied cold water to drink and no other prisoners were allowed in his cell, which denied him socialization. He wanted to talk to the Gay Liberation guys to see if they could help him with his prison problems.

He continually asked for favors from the guards and fellow prisoners. The guards were not kind to Swindler, and his access to water was restricted. His food was served last after it had grown cold. He was denied religious services, he said, and he was not allowed to walk and thus get exercise. He continually complained that his cell was either too hot or cold, depending upon the weather. He kept waiting for someone to mention the phone calls, but no one did.

Court officials providing newly purchased safety precautions at Swindler's trial.

CHAPTER TWENTY-FOUR

The Sebastian County Courtroom was a massive room with two story windows and paneled mahogany walls. The jury sat on the right side of the room in solemn black chairs, and the judge sat on a raised platform. The Arkansas flag was to his right, and the American flag was to his left. The court clerk box was below on the left, and the witness stand was on the right.

Directly across the room from the jury was a long bench next to an exquisitely paneled door. Behind that fancy door was a holding cell with steel bars. Back in the 1930s, inmates were brought down from the jail in an elevator with thick bars.

When the presiding judge hit his gavel and called the room to order, the sound was amplified and caused everyone to sit up a little straighter.

For the Swindler murder trial, the courtroom was the province of Judge Holland, who was presiding over his first murder trial. Judge Holland was a tall, slender man with a kind face. He had the reputation of being fair to both sides, but was not the kind of judge who hung out with attorneys in the local judicial hangout bar or on the golf course.

He advised the jury that they were being good citizens by serving.

"This trial will be one that will cause you a few sleepless nights. You must listen attentively, take notes with the paper and pencil provided to you, refrain from chewing gum, and do not discuss the case with anyone, not even the person who sits on either side of you in the jury box. Don't talk about this case with your husband or wife, your best friend, or with your beautician or barber."

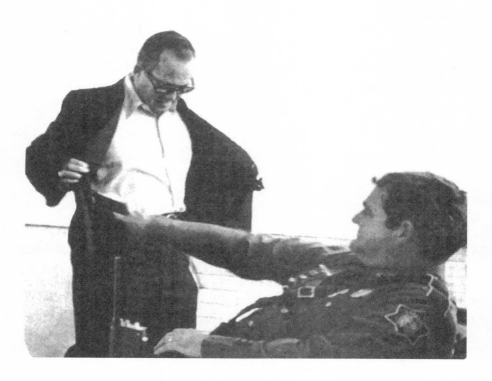

Cindy's father, Odell Davis, a retired policeman, being searched and scanned before entering the courtroom.

Cindy and her daddy made plans to go to the trial. She wanted to see the scumbag who killed her husband, the father of a three-month-old little girl, and the step-father to her other children.

Cindy had been nervously waiting for the trial to start. She wanted to stare right through Swindler, and she hoped he would look at her just once.

"I just want to see if I can stare him down," she told her dad. "You know, see if I can make him squirm."

Cindy and her daddy parked a block away because the courthouse would be packed on the first day of actual testimony. Cindy clutched her coat tightly around her neck and held onto her daddy's arm, partly for stability and partly for warmth. The courthouse was only a few blocks east of the Arkansas River, and the wind was strong. They climbed up the concrete steps to the entrance and pushed open the glass doors. Deputies were checking in everyone with a new contraption that would beep if it registered a gun or a knife or anything metallic that could be used to harm someone.

A photographer for the newspaper took a shot of Cindy's dad being examined, and it appeared in the next morning's newspaper.

The bailiff had already opened the courtroom door. Cindy and her dad chose an aisle seat on a wooden bench on the left side of the courtroom. The first thing Cindy noticed were various initials and dates carved into the seats and on the backs of the seats in front of them.

She poked her dad with her right elbow and nodded for him to see the carvings.

He smiled and took her hand. He whispered, "It shows a hell of a lack of respect for the judicial system."

The courtroom filled quickly. The court reporter, who was a woman, entered followed by the circuit clerk, a man, and then the prosecutors,

Charles Karr and Ron Fields. Mr. Karr and Mr. Fields had visited often with Cindy, and they both looked around until they saw her. Once they did, they mouthed hello and smiled.

The two lawyers who had been appointed to represent Swindler then came in. Cindy knew their names because she had read about them in the newspaper. She knew they were doing their job, but she didn't like the looks of Don Langston or Hubert Graves.

When John Swindler was brought in by the bailiff, there were gasps in the courtroom. He had a noticeable limp from where Randy had shot him in his left thigh.

He sat down at a long table where his attorneys sat.

Cindy had a perfect view of him, but instead of staring at him, she looked away, afraid she'd cry or throw up. She didn't know which.

And then the jury was brought in. Their names had already been published in the paper, following their selection. She recognized Mrs. Shuffield, a beautiful dark-haired woman whose husband was the administrator of Sparks Hospital. Cindy didn't know her, but she had heard her speak at a meeting at her church.

The bailiff announced, "All rise," in a booming voice when Judge Holland entered the courtroom. Once the judge sat down, the bailiff, once again in a loud voice, said, "Be seated and come to order."

A cleaned-up Swindler is led into Sebastian County Courtroom for his trial.

CHAPTER TWENTY-FIVE

The courtroom crowd seemed stunned that a man shot in the stomach two times would be strong enough to fire his revolver at the defendant.

The court appointed attorney, Don Langston, then presented the defendant's side of the story which was simply that the officer shot first and the defendant shot back in self-defense.

At that, Cindy got up and left, her low black heels clicking on the wooden floor. She felt everyone in the courtroom watching her leave. She didn't cry at all. It was a case of being too mad to cry.

The judge raised his gavel and hit it once and called for quiet in the courtroom. If anyone was watching John Swindler, they would have seen a wide smile cross his face.

The next person to testify was Carl Tinder, a good-looking gray-haired man. He was tall and held himself straight. When he walked to the stand, anyone could tell he was a man of confidence. He gave his name and address and said he'd lived all his life in Fort Smith. After answering some perfunctory questions about where he worked and where it was located, he told the prosecutor that he was acquainted with Randy Basnett for about four years.

"If Randy was working the North side of town, he nearly always came in for a Coke in the afternoon or coffee in the morning. I really enjoyed visiting with Officer Basnett for the few minutes we shared a beverage in the office."

He then answered the questions put to him by Karr and told how a big bushy-haired man came in and asked for directions, and he and Randy told him how to get to Alma and Highway 71 to Kansas City.

He then told that Randy Basnett left and so did the man who was lost.

"I was behind the counter, and I could see Basnett climb into his car, look at his clipboard, and pick up his radio. Basnett then moved his police car about ten feet to the rear of the gold car. He climbed out of his car and casually walked over to Swindler, who had his head under the hood. Basnett must have asked for Swindler's identification because he put the hood down and walked to the driver's side of the car. Randy followed him every step of the way."

The prosecutor asked how Swindler entered the car, and Mr. Tinder said, "With his face looking out the windshield. Suddenly he pulled a revolver and shot the officer two times in the stomach and chest. Randy screamed when he fell down."

"I couldn't believe it," Mr. Tinder said. "I just couldn't believe it. As Randy was falling, he pulled his pistol and unloaded it at Swindler's side of the car."

Mr. Tinder was clearly shaken by the events he was re-living. "Anyway, I ran out and Swindler was having trouble getting his car started. I hoped he'd get it started because if he didn't, he would come after me."

Don Langston objected to the last statement and Judge Holland agreed with Langston and sustained the objection. He told the jury not to pay any attention to what Mr. Tinder had said. For the rest of the trial if a lawyer objected to something said in court, and the judge sustained the objection, then he felt he needn't explain it to the jury every time. If there was an objection, and the judge didn't agree, then he said, "Overruled."

The jury looked at each other as if to say, "I learned all about this on television. If a lawyer makes an objection, and the judge agrees, then he would say 'sustained.'"

The judge saw several of the women jurists roll their eyes. "I'm sure many of you are familiar with this legal jargon because you watch a lot of crime shows."

The jury laughed and the ladies who had rolled their eyes tried to disappear into their chairs.

The judge hit his gavel again. "Continue, Mr. Tinder."

"Anyway, I ran out. Finally, Swindler got his car started, and he drove out of the driveway flying. Across the street, I saw a trooper stick his head out the door. I hollered "Shoot him"as loud as I could.

"As best I remember, he unloaded his pistol on him. I couldn't go to Randy right then because he was lying flat on the ground with his pistol still in his hand, still cocked, and his hand was waving around and around with it. So, I waited a few minutes till he got his hand straight, and then I ran toward him and grabbed his arm and laid his arm down to his side and taken the pistol out of his hand. Then I worked with him, I'd say ten minutes, trying to keep him alive, and that's all I know."

Mr. Langston continued questioning, and Carl Tinder seemed exhausted at reliving these dark moments of his life: witnessing a murder, hiding out from someone who threatened to kill him and his wife if he testified in court, and actually sitting up in the witness chair and describing what happened on September 24, 1976.

"The ambulance came and taken him to the hospital," Carl Tinder continued. "I knew what his condition was because I worked in the funeral business twenty-eight years, and his eyes was already set when I got to him. He was still breathing, but the breathing was from the lungs, that's all. There just wasn't no hope for him at all."

CHAPTER TWENTY-SIX

Steve Cardwell was called to testify on behalf of the state. He said he and his wife dropped by the convenience store for a few things after work at the Southwest Times Record.

"I went in to get a few items, and my wife waited in the car. We must have arrived just shortly before the shooting began. I got my items, and as I was leaving, the shooting began between Swindler and Officer Basnett."

Cardwell pulled a white Kleenex from his shirt pocket and began to wipe his brow. "When I got safely back to my car, my wife was hysterical. She had heard the shots and was afraid I was killed."

Mr. Cardwell ended his testimony by saying, "I heard the officer's scream. I've never before heard such an agonizing scream."

Next up was Highway Patrolman Charles Lambert. He testified that he had worked for the Highway Patrol since June of 1976, and he was now assigned to the Narcotics Division.

"I had come from Fayetteville, down Highway 71 South, and I was going to the state headquarters on Kelley Highway in Fort Smith to pick up some information. Just prior to getting off the Kelley Highway exit, I passed a car, a yellowish-gold-colored Duster, and observed the defendant driving this car."

Prosecutor Karr asked Lambert how he usually dressed.

"I usually wear Levis and a blouse-type shirt. I let my hair grow long and have a full beard. I usually wear a headband. I try to dress like I'm a drug dealer."

"What was your assignment that day?"

"I was going to Fort Smith to do some undercover work."

Prosecutor Karr breathed deeply. "On your way to headquarters did you observe a gold Plymouth with South Carolina tags?"

"I did and the man driving it looked like the people I have to arrest."

"Do you see that man in the courtroom today?"

Charles Lambert pointed to a very large red-headed man who looked like he might have had SIN carved on his forehead.

Lambert said when he went into the police building, he looked across the street and saw the same car he'd passed earlier.

"I thought to myself that was a coincidence, but I filed that away and went back to doing what I came to do.'

"I happened to look out the window again, and that's when I heard the gunfire. I ran for my briefcase, and I took my revolver out. I went outside, shooting at the gold car as it sped down Kelley. I watched it cross the interstate, and head down a little dirt road that leads to the river. I then got into my Volkswagen I was assigned and headed in pursuit. A city policeman drove up in his patrol car, and I flagged him down. I got into the car, but it stalled out. We then ran to Basnett's car, got in, and started it up, and then it died. But we got it started and took off on Kelley, crossed the 540 bridge and went down a road down toward the river."

"And were you able to follow the car?" Mr. Karr asked.

"There were fresh tracks for us to follow. And then we saw a man standing beside a bulldozer, and he pointed the way for us to go."

Karr asked Lambert to identify certain landmarks on photographs for the jury. Lambert identified the place where he and Ross found the gold car nosed out in some heavy brush.

"We heard the defendant screaming that he wanted to give up, that he didn't want to die, please don't kill me."

When the defendant's attorney questioned Lambert, he tried to make a case that the sun would have gotten in Lambert's eyes so he couldn't see clearly what was going on at the service station in front of him, and that there would have been glares off the plate glass windows.

The defense attorney also asked Lambert if he saw who shot first. Lambert answered that he heard two shots in rapid succession and then heard five or six. He couldn't positively testify where the bullets came from.

It was the defense's theory that Randy Basnett fired first, and that Swindler only fired in self-defense. The fact that Officer Lambert didn't lie to make a stronger case for the state was a real testament to his integrity as a policeman and as a gentleman.

Other officers testified to what they heard on the police radio and how they responded. Major Rivaldo played the tape of the radio call by Officer Basnett to police headquarters. But before he played the tape he was asked to explain to the jurors what various police codes meant, such as: 10-4 Yes, I understand; 10-6 Busy; 10-20. What's your location?

Major Rivaldo played the tape that revealed Officer Basnett's voice. The courtroom was very quiet. It seemed that all were honoring the policeman killed in the line of duty.

Major Rivaldo knew that his testimony would be difficult to listen to, especially when the radio calls gave a play-by-play dialogue of the events beginning with Randy Basnett's call to headquarters to say that he had just spotted a gold Plymouth Duster with a South Carolina license plate.

Basnett knew that it was driven by a man who was armed and dangerous. What he had no way of knowing was that another policeman in South Carolina had said he felt sorry for any lawman who tried to arrest Swindler.

CHAPTER TWENTY-SEVEN

Judge Holland grew weary of all of Langston's motions for a new trial. It seemed that Langston filed motions left and right, but to no avail.

Langston said his client could not get a fair trial in Fort Smith because of all the publicity. Holland was dead set on keeping the trial in his Sebastian County Circuit Courthouse. The attorneys for Swindler even asked for a directed verdict of acquittal and a change from capital murder to second degree murder. Once again, Judge Holland said no.

Perhaps the most interesting testimony came from Randy Basnett's friend and fellow policeman:

He was questioned by Charles Karr:

Q. State your name for the jury, please.

A. Robert Ross.

Q. Where do you live, Mr. Ross?

A. 5801 Kinkead.

Q. How are you employed?

A. By the Fort Smith Police Department.

Q. In what capacity?

A. Patrolman.

Q. How long have you been with the police department?

A. Seven years.

Q. And were you working for the police department on September 24, 1976?

A. Yes, sir.

Q. What was your assignment that day?

A. I was on patrol duty at that time.

Q. And what troop were you on?

A. Troop One.

Q. I refer you to that Friday, September 24,1976, and ask if you recall that date?

A. I do, sir.

Q. Do you recall what shift you were working?

A. Yes, sir, the afternoon shift.

Q. What were the hours of that shift?

A. From 1:15 to 9:15

Q. What car were you assigned to that day?

A. Car three.

Q. And generally, where is that beat?

A. That beat funs from Kelley north to the Van Buren side.

Q. Were you working alone in that car at that time?

A. Yes, sir.

Q. I refer you to sometime shortly after 5:00 o'clock on that Friday afternoon, and did you receive an assignment at that time?

A. Yes, sir. I had received a call approximately that time that Office

Basnett was stopping a vehicle that we had been looking for that came out in briefing. I received a call to back this unit up. I was approximately at the intersection of Midland and Kelley. I did turn right and proceeded to that location.

Q. Okay. Now you received a call to back up Officer Basnett, and what location was given to you at that time?

A. It was in the 5800 block of Kelley, the Roadrunner Gas and Food Service at this location.

Q. And you were at Midland and Kelley and you say you turned around.

A. Yes.

Q. All right. And how did you go then? What was your direction of travel?

A. Okay. I made a U-turn just a little south of the intersection, with emergency lights and siren, I did proceed back east on Kelley Highway.

Q. And would you tell the jury then, what happened as you drove down Kelley and what did you did next, please?

A. Yes, sir. As I was proceeding east on the back-up assignment, I had approximately got to the 5700 block and I received information that shots had been fired. Upon rolling into the northwest entrance to the Roadrunner Market, I heard—there came over the radio Officer had been shot. As I rolled up into the service driveway, I did observe as I opened the vehicle's left side door, I did observe Officer Basnett lying on his back.

Q. And what did you do then, Mr. Ross?

A. At this time, my unit did die. I was kind of shocked at the time I had looked over toward the officer's body. About this time Trooper Lambert did open the vehicle's door, it did draw my attention to him.

He did show me—he was identifying himself as he was getting into the vehicle. He had a Chief's Special small .38 revolver in his hand, ejecting the shells out of it, telling me he had fired rounds at the gold Duster in question. He was telling me the direction that the vehicle had left. I did try to get the unit started. It would not start. We did jump out of my unit, Unit Three. I did grab my shotgun and ran to Unit Four. It was parked off, just a little west of where my vehicle was. I did get into Officer Basnett's vehicle, threw the briefcase out, and started the unit up. Officer Lambert was with me. I did proceed out to Kelley. Unit Four died there. We had to—took us a few more seconds to get it started. Then we proceeded east across the overpass.

Q. Did you ever go over to Randy?

A. I did not.

Q. Was he dressed in his police uniform at that time?

A. Yes, sir. He was.

Q. Could you tell anything about his condition there?

A. The only thing I could tell was that he had been shot twice.

Q. Were there any other people around or anything?

A. Not at this time, no.

Q. Then, what did you do, Mr. Ross?

A. We proceeded on over the overpass. The vehicle was headed toward the bottoms, the river district. So, we proceeded on. There was an access road where the new excavation work was going on, and they do plant crops down in this area also. I did know the area. We proceeded on east. You could tell where the vehicle was going by the sway in the dirt. The vehicle was traveling at a very high rate of speed. We did proceed on down and we noticed some excavation work going on. There was a man standing out in a clearing area by a couple of big brush piles pointing in that direction. I guess you would say south.

Q. Let me interrupt you there and ask you a question. Could you see at this time the car you were pursuing?

A. No, sir.

Q. Had you ever seen it, in fact?

A. Not at this point, no.

Q. Now you said that you had been down in this area before and you were somewhat familiar with it?

A. Yes, sir.

Q. Then what did you do?

A. There were two big brush piles. We proceeded to, I would, say the second brush pile. Then there was a short clearing before it got to the wooded area. We did park the unit just on the other side of the brush pile. We were leery of an ambush. The man could have parked on the other side. We did check this out, and we did note where the vehicle had proceeded on over to another small, I'll say dirt, road that went down to a recreation area, camping area or picnic area, whatever you'd rather refer to it.

Q. Had you ever been to that recreation area before, the area you're talking about?

A. Yes, sir.

Q. Describe that road a little bit.

A. The road is just barely wide enough for a car to get down. It's very dense, a lot of brush, and it is this way for approximately a quarter of a mile. We did drive our vehicle up onto this road. We both did partially open our doors due to the dense undergrowth because it was an ideal set-up for an ambush. We did proceed slowly down this road until we came to another clearing where a picnic table, a little outhouse, and a few other things were that I can't recall at this time. We parked the vehicle just at the edge of this and proceeded to search.

Q. All right. Now had you entered this little picnic area at that time?

A. Not at that time. We parked the car just to the edge of it. We didn't want to drive just right into this open area. We thought that would be foolish. I did get out. Took my shotgun. Officer Lambert got out of the vehicle. At approximately this time Trooper Hutchins did drive up behind my vehicle. We had started. I went to my left and Trooper Lambert went to my right. Trooper Hutchins took a point of lead. We did search the area. I was along the river bank and had just come up short. And Trooper Hutchins stated that he thought he'd seen the vehicle. I had swung around and I did see the vehicle. I hollered at Hutchins, "I see the vehicle and the car door is open." I told him I would cover him if he got to the small outhouse. He did make a dash for it. I moved on into the woods to provide better cover.

Q. All right. Now where was this car at the time you saw it there?

A. Okay. It was like in a recessed area. The man had drove the vehicle up a, looked like a mound of dirt, grass, and overgrowth had over-taken it. He drove the vehicle up over this and the car, like repelled and dropped on in that recessed area.

Q. I show you the photograph that has been marked State's Exhibit 13, and ask if you recognize that?

A. I do, sir. That is the vehicle I did observe at the scene. It is the gold Duster that we had on briefing with the South Carolina tags.

Q. What did you do then, Mr. Ross?

A. Okay. Just as we had observed the vehicle and Hutchins had taken cover, I did—we all did hear a man hollering in the woods. Was hollering, 'Don't shoot. Don't kill me. I give up.'

Q. Could you not see anyone at that time?

A. I did not see anyone at this time.

Q. Were you in the woods at that time or were you still in the clearing?

A. I had stepped off into the brush, the brushy area. I was still at this position when the man started hollering.

Q. Then what did you do?

A. I hollered at Hutchins. I told him we better proceed with caution. The man could be setting us up. So, we kept our same formation or you might say position. We proceeded toward the man hollering very carefully.

Q. Had you seen him by this time?

A. Not yet.

W. Go ahead.

A. We proceeded on maybe twenty yards, and we could still hear him hollering. He stated that he had been wounded. He wanted to give up. Still hollering all along. I did move up and I did observe him with his hands around a tree, high above this time. We all halted. Sergeant Phillips, who was to my right hollered, "His hands are in the air. Don't shoot." So we proceeded on to the man. As I approached him, he started to drop his hands. At this time I did strike him in the ribs with the butt of my shotgun. He did fall to the ground and we did handcuff him at this time. Then, at this time, we were all excited, and we did verbally read his rights to him.

Q. Okay. Now who actually handcuffed him?

A. It was I and Officer Hutchins.

Q. And was that after he was on the ground?

A. Well, after we had done this, we were all concerned about the weapons. The man wouldn't say, but he just motioned with his head over in a direction. I paid no more attention to that. The man was placed under arrest and we started to go toward the vehicle.

Q. Okay, now who is we?

A. Me, Officer Hutchins and, I believe, Charlie Brunck was to the rear of the man. I'm not real sure, I'm pretty sure.

Q. Which vehicle? Now are you talking about ...

A. It would be Unit Four. The one that I had drove down in there. I did place him in that car at this time, and we had to wait till someone came before we could get all the vehicles cleared out. Captain Bettis was there and other supervisors, and I remember I did get the order to take the man to the hospital.

Q. Where did you place him in your car?

A. In the rear of my vehicle.

Q. Describe what kind of car that is.

A. It's a regular police vehicle with the screen—the back seat is screened off. The doors have the back handles off so the prisoner can't get away. The doors were shut and the traffic was cleared so I proceeded to the hospital. As I was driving, I did take my Miranda card out of my shirt pocket and I did read his rights again in the car. I asked him if he understood his rights and he said yes.

Q. Did anyone else go with you?

A. No. I was by myself.

Q. Did anyone else go with you in their vehicle?

A. Yes. Officer Brunk followed in a unit behind me.

Q. Now by the time you actually got him back to your car, there were other officers at the scene?

A. Yes.

Q. And you say some of them were parked behind you and you had to wait until they cleared the road before you could get out. Is that correct?

A. Yes, sir.

Q. Do you recall the direction of travel to the hospital?

A. Yes, sir. I do. It was back down Kelley, which would be in a west direction. At the intersection of Midland and Kelley, I did make a left which would be south. I followed Midland to 10th Street on Short Towson. Towson straight out to North "H" Street, City Emergency Room Exit.

Q. And you took him there to the hospital?

A. Yes, sir. I did.

Q. And Officer Brunk was behind you?

A. Yes, sir. He was.

Q. Who took the defendant into the hospital?

A. There were other people there. There was some emergency room attendants and a few other officers. They did assist the man out of the car and into the emergency room.

Q. Did you stay at the hospital for any time?

A. Yes, sir. I did.

Q. How long were you there? Do you know?

A. Approximately maybe two hours.

Q. Were you present during any of the time that the defendant was being treated or anything?

A. Yes, sir. I was there in the emergency room with him as they took his clothes off and got him ready for the X-rays, prepared him.

Q. Okay. And were there other officers there at the time?

A. Yes, sir. A number of officers.

Q. And then, after you left the hospital, where did you go?

A. I went back to the police station.

Q. And how did you leave the hospital?

A. I did leave by Unit Four. I drove Officer Basnett's unit back to the station.

Q. Okay, and did you find anything there in the car at that time?

A. Yes, sir. I found on a clipboard, he did have the briefing notes that had come out and it did have Swindler's vehicle description, license plate number on it.

Q. And that was in Officer Basnett's personal notebook?

A. It's like a clipboard. His briefing notes were set right to my right where you could see them. In plain sight.

Q. And then did you turn that in down at the Police Department when you got there.

A. Yes, sir. I did. Yes, sir. Along with his hat.

Mr. Karr: No further questions.

CHAPTER TWENTY-EIGHT

When Mr. Ross was cross-examined by the defendant's co-council, Mr. Don Langston, it was evident by his questions that he was trying to get Officer Ross to declare that Randy Basnett did not follow the procedure as to how to apprehend or arrest someone who is standing outside their vehicle.

You should never let them get back in the car.

Attorney Langston was hinting that it was Randy's fault that he was killed.

But Mr. Ross was a good friend of Randy's. He wasn't going to defile his name or the position he held in the police force. His stock answer to Langston's question was, "It depends on the situation."

Langston also questioned Ross about the use of his shotgun to restrain the defendant. And he also wanted to know if he put his foot on the defendant's neck when he handcuffed him while he was on the ground. Ross denied that, and he said he didn't see any police officer hit or kick the defendant or use unusual force in apprehending the man.

Another witness called was Troy Marvin Farrar.

Q. Where do you live, Mr. Farrar?

A. 2900 Russell here in Fort Smith.

Q. For whom do you work?

A. Kenneth Allen.

Q. What type of work is that?

A. I'm a heavy equipment operator.

Q. I refer you to last September, specifically, September 24, 1976, and ask you if you were working down in the river bottoms at the end of Kelley Highway at that time?

A. Yes. I was.

Q. What kind of work were you doing down there?

A. I was operating a loader.

Q. For what type of work.

A. I was loading dump trucks as they came in and out.

Q. All right, sir. I refer you to sometime in the afternoon shortly after five o'clock, and ask you if you recall an incident that occurred down there at that time.

A. Yes. You're talking about the fellow coming down so fast in the car?

Q. All right. If you would, in your own words, explain to the jury what happened right before the car came by and right afterwards?

A. Well, I didn't have much business and I was just standing by my loader doing nothing and saw this car coming, and I watched it as it came down the road, you know, and around the corner and come by me. I couldn't say how fast it was going, but he was moving on and went right on by me and appeared to be going to run the car into the bushes, but when he got to the trees where he was going to go there was a road. So, down—he went down the road.

Q. Had you ever been down that road before?

A. Yes sir, I had.

Q. Did you know where it goes?

A. Yes. It just goes down just a little way further to a little camp area we've got down there.

Q. Now you say, how fast was the car traveling?

A. Oh, fast enough til it would jump and wouldn't leave tracks.

Q. What do you mean by that?

A. Well, when it hit a little bump or something it would just jump and leave a two- or three-foot space there where the car wouldn't even leave a track.

Q. You mean at certain times, it was completely airborne?

A. Right.

Q. And then what was the next thing you saw?

A. Well, I was thinking about telling him he wasn't supposed to be there. I'm glad I didn't. I kept watching back up the road, then I saw the lights of the police car, you know, coming, and when they got close enough, well, I showed them which way he went. They went on down and followed him up.

Q. Were there any cars or any other people down there or anything like that?

A. No, not that late in the evening.

Q. Is that private property down there?

A. Yes, it is.

Q. How many police cars came down there?

A. Fifteen. At first there was only one and they blocked the road where it went through the trees. They blocked the road for a few minutes, and when they seen the other officers coming up by, of course, went on down, waiting for back-up, I guess. Then immediately there was about fifteen more.

Q. Did you hear shots fired down there?

A. No, I didn't.

Q. No other questions.

There were other witnesses called by the prosecution, and during one questioning, Don Langston asked to approach the bench. He told the judge that his client needed some nerve pills that he had been prescribed. He was about to "flip out" and could someone go up to his cell to get the pills?

The judge granted permission.

CHAPTER TWENTY-NINE

On Friday, February 25, 1977, Swindler took the stand. He still had long red hair, but he'd been cleaned up. He asked for his sun glasses which had been taken upon his arrest. Holland granted that request, but he did not allow the ankle guard to be taken off Swindler's leg.

John Edward Swindler put his hand on the Bible and swore to tell the truth. (Of course that really didn't hold much weight because Swindler claimed to worship Satan.)

His attorney, Don Langston began the direct examination of his client.

Q. State your name for the jury.

A. John Edward Swindler

Q. How old are you, Mr. Swindler?

A. Thirty-two.

Q. Where and when were you born?

A. May 12, 1944.

Q. And where?

A. Richland County, Columbia, South Carolina.

Q. Are your parents living?

A. They're deceased. Both of them.

Q. When did your father die?

A. First part of 1970.

Q. And your mother?

A. 1969.

Q. How many brothers and sisters did you have?

A. That I have living now or all told?

Q. That were born.

A. There's thirteen in my family.

Q. How many are still living?

A. I have one sister and there's five boys.

Q. Did you grow up in Columbia, South Carolina?

A. Yes, sir.

Q. Did you attend any church while you were there growing up?

A. Oakwood Presbyterian Church, Monticello Road, Columbia.

Q. Did your mother have anything to do with the church there?

A. She was a Sunday School teacher and grew up in the church herself.

Q. Did you have anything to do with the church besides attend?

A. I sat in once in a while in the choir. To fill in if someone was sick.

Q. Have you been able to contact your people since this event occurred?

A. No, sir. I have not.

Q. Why is that? Because you've been in jail?

A. Yes, sir.

Q. And were you allowed to make any long distance phone calls?

A. No. I wasn't allowed.

Q. Let's go back to September 24th of 1976? Were you traveling here in Arkansas?

A. I came through. Yes, sir.

Q. Where were you going?

A. Kansas City, Kansas.

Q. What were you going up there for?

A. To see some friends, sorta stay out of sight for a while.

Q. You have some friends up there?

A. Well, yes, sir. I've pulled time with quite a number of people.

Q. All right. Did you have a road map with you?

A. Yes, sir. I did.

Q. Now, as I understand it, you cannot read. Is that correct?

A. That's right.

Q. Can you write?

A. Yes, sir.

Q. How much can you write?

A. I can write anything you want me to write.

Q. And read it after you write it?

A. Well, I mean, I can read it to a very limited extent, yes, but far as following a map, numbers, I have no problem, and if something's wrote down, of course, I can find it, if it's on the map.

Q. Now how were you able to follow this to come through Arkansas?

A. A hitchhiker happened to mark out a map and leave it in my possession.

Q. All right. There is a mark here on it at Alma, Highway 71. Who placed that mark there?

A. A young man I picked up for a hitchhiker.

Q. Had you told him where you were going or something?

A. Not at that time, a little bit later on, well, he had an atlas and then he said well, I think I have a spare map, too, you know, so then he got the map and he says, if you run me by my place, I'll even help you out, you know, to the effect that map you out a route that you can follow.

Q. All right, now, then did he mark this here at Alma?

A. Yes.

O. On Highway 71?

A. Yes, to the best of my knowledge.

Q. Was that where you intended to turn? Was that where you intended to turn north?

A. On 71?

Q. Yes.

A. Yes, I did.

Q. All right, now these road signs that give these town names, can you read those?

A. Well, I can read them, but every time I'd pass by I'd be, the map was with the line, well, you know, well, I'd just turn the map over with my finger, and I'd be able to follow.

Q. Are you telling me you could follow the dots on a map?

A. Yes, sir.

Q. And not the names?

A. Oh, well, I could follow the names to an extent, you know what I'm saying, but I would have to—

Q. All right, now do you know when you got to Alma where you were supposed to turn, did you notice that or anything?

A. No, sir. I was supposed to turn on 71 and I had left that morning from Monroe, Louisiana and right before coming to Fort Smith, for which I did not know where I was supposed to turn on 71, you see, and somehow or another had my head turned and I passed that.

Q. Did you have intentions of coming to Fort Smith?

A. No, I did not.

Q. Now when you were traveling, did you know that any bulletins were out about you?

A. I did know I was a suspect, yes, sir.

Q. And how did you find that out?

A. I was on Main Street, the last block of Main before getting to the capitol and someone who I pulled time frequently before in fact, I think several times, approached me and said "Swindler, I don't know if you know it or not, but I heard that you are wanted. And I said "Not me. I just got out." And this was on Wednesday and I had just got out on the 17th which was the Friday before, and so he went on to tell me, said, "Yes, it's an outstanding murder charge," and I said, "Not me."

Q. Did you call anyone about that?

A. Well, I had been drinking at the time and so he got me off the main street and I got around to the side and then I called the City Police Department and asked the City Police Department and they said they didn't have no outstanding warrants for someone right then, you know what I'm saying, so then I called the Sheriff's Department and asked them and the Sheriff's Department said "Yeah, we've got outstanding warrants," but I didn't give 'em my name, see, but I said, "Could you tell me who the outstanding warrant of murder might be? And he said, "What's your name?" and I said, "I don't have no name." And I said, "I'm just concerned," and he says, "I don't know which one you're referring to and I'm not allowed to tell you if I could."

Q. And did this cause you some concern?

A. Well, yes, it did, and so—like I'd been drinking a little bit.

Q. All right, now then, when you got that—After you had driven a while, did you then notice that you were on the wrong road, after you passed Alma, Highway 71, did you notice?

A. Oh? You're going to jump from—yes, sir.

Q. All the time you were traveling through Arkansas, did you have it in your mind about these bulletins about you?

A. Yes, sir. There was a CB radio in the Duster which I was driving and I was spotted, I can't say what town, can't hardly say what state, but I assume it was pretty close to Georgia, and so I heard on the radio, and so, therefore, I got off. I kept, just kept bearing to the right just about every time I came to a highway trying to get away, my intention I had of going to Florida fleeing after I heard that they had a warrant on me and I had called several people to the effect, you know, to try to help me out and they just told me to lay low and they would try to do the best they can to try to find out what was going on, you see, because I thought at the time that I was being framed to the effect I had just been released out of prison.

Q. All right. When you ... Now did you notice on your map any town such as that, like Fort Smith here?

A. What you mean, large?

Q. Larger than just dots. Did you notice any towns such as that, like Fort Smith here?

A. Oh, yeah. Fort Smith, yes.

Q. Did you notice that?

A. I know right before I got to Fort Smith they was a circle around it to the effect I was supposed to have turned right before getting to Fort Smith, well, so, when I seen the sign, Fort Smith, on the map and then the road sign out there, Fort Smith, I knew I'd already been past where I was supposed to turn.

Q. So then what did you decide to do?

A. I just took the next exit and pulled into the gas station.

Q. What did you do when you pulled up?

A. Well, I pulled right up to the door just about, passing the door, you could see the back of my car, of course, but I got out.

Q. Just a moment, did you see a police unit there when you drove up?

A. No, I did not.

Q. Could you have read the word "police?"

A. No, I cannot.

Q. So you did not see a police unit there?

A. No, I did not.

Q. What did you observe outside when you drove up, if you observed anything? Any other vehicles there?

A. No, I did not.

Q. Was there any at the gas pumps?

A. There was none at the gas pumps. There might have been some parked on the side but there was no emblem to recognize them to be a policeman. If it was just wrote on there, I couldn't of read it anyway.

Q. All right. You pulled your car, where?

A. I pulled it up to the front, just to where you barely could see the back.

Q. In what direction were you pointing? East or west?

A. Well, as I come off of, I believe it was Highway 40, and turned on Kelley Highway, then I pulled past the pumps and then made a U-turn and pulled back up in front of the front door of the filling station and the grocery store combined together.

Q. With the front of your car pointing toward the Interstate highway?

A. That's right.

Q. All right. Then what happened?

A. Well, I grabbed—

Q. What was your purpose in stopping at the service station?

A. For directions only.

Q. Did you intend to buy any gas or anything?

A. No, sir.

Q. All right.

A. I had a full tank.

Q. When you got out of the car, did you have this map with you.

A. Yes, sir, I picked up the map and I walked into the filling station and grocery store combined together and after I got inside and I was showing the man who run the grocery store—

Q. Did he testify here earlier?

A. Yes, he did. Well, I says I must have lost my way—

Q. Did you take this map out and show it?

A. I had it in my hand, yes. And I asked him to show me where I made my mistake.

Q. And did you see the policeman then?

A. Then the policeman walked up behind me and said something like, "Son, what's your problem?" I had the road map in my hand, and I said, "Sir, I've lost my way. I'm going to Kansas City."

Q. So the police officer—

A. I don't remember exactly which one said, "Well, you see, there's not much difference." He says, "It's only a few miles back." And then he says,, "Where're you coming from, son?" and I said, "Columbia, South Carolina," you know.

Q. Did Mr. Tinder who testified here, did he do anything to show you anything on the map?

A. Well, both of them together sorta tried to explain. I says, "I can't read," you know.

Q. Did you finally understand where they were pointing to?

A. Yes, I did.

Q. Then did you decide to leave?

A. Well, yes sir, and I said "Thank you." And I walked out got in the car, and the car had been running hot off and on because I'd been pushing it pretty strong and as I cranked it up—

Q. Did you see the policeman come out of the building?

A. No, I did not.

Q. When you went into the store, did you have anything on you?

A. Oh, yes. I carried two revolvers at that time.

Q. Where did you have them?

A. I had one underneath my belt and one in my pocket. Neither one of them was visible.

Q. Did you have your shirt down over them?

A. Yes, I did.

Q. All right. You went back to your car?

A. Yes, I did.

Q. Then what happened?

A. I cranked up the car and I seen a red light come on and then, of course, I noticed the car was hot, so I pulled it out there where some pumps were there. Instead of pulling all the way out, I just backed up a few feet to where there was a middle aisle of pumps, in other words, the first pumps of the station. I got out of the car, raised the hood and of course, I shut off the car. I checked the oil first. And it seemed all right. So I got back in the car and I cranked it up, then I went up and checked the water.

Q. Now, at this time, did the police officer come out of the building, to your knowledge?

A. No, he did not.

Q. Could he have? And you just not seen him?

A. Now, he could of, but I did not see him at that time, no.

Q. All right, continue.

A. All right, I raised, I mean, I checked the water and I couldn't see no water in it so, Like I say, when I checked the oil, I opened the cap is what I meant and I didn't see no water in it and it was steaming sorta, so then I got back in the car to keep from putting water in a hot radiator, I cranked up the car, walked back to the front and put water in it and put the cap back on and let the hood down, then come around and started to get in the car. Well, I had my left hand on the door of the window of the car, my right foot was in the car, and while I'm in the car, well, I usually take the revolver that's got underneath my belt out and I had passed so many policemen before that at that time, well, like a State Trooper right before had told me in a park down the street, you know, so, therefore, I didn't think I was wanted or that car was wanted up this way and so really it didn't upset me seeing this police officer in the place, you know, walking up behind me, so I pulled the gun out and started to lay it down and the car was running and so just as I started to lay the gun, the .38 snub-nose on the front seat, well, then I heard a cock, you know.

Q. Did you hear anybody say anything to you?

A. Something to the effect, you hippie, you know, you understand what I'm saying.

Q. Then you heard a gun cock?

A. I was fixing to lay the revolver on the front seat. And about this time, I heard a gun cock and I mean real close and before I could get my head around somebody done shot me in the side or in the leg, I couldn't tell which one was first because the two bullets were fired instant and so I just turned on around and defended myself after being shot by somebody who I did not know at the time, split of a second, I shot and as he was falling I did see that he was a policeman.

Basically, Swindler claimed he shot in self-defense. He also testified that when he was arrested after the shooting, he was beaten up by several officers who arrived at the scene of his arrest. "Before I was handcuffed, they asked me where the guns was at. I nodded my head where they was at."

When his attorney asked if anyone hit him, he said, "I got sorta touched up a little bit. By hands and feet and a rifle butt or shotgun butt, and what-not.

"I also got my lip busted up, not only by a fist or two, but after I was on the ground, they kicked me in the mouth, loosened up my teeth, tearing my gums loose. Two people jumped on top of me, and I was abused at that time by kicking and hitting and what-have-you. Then one man put a shotgun in my mouth and said I better hope that the policeman I shot don't die. He said that if he did, he was going to blow a hole in the back side of my head.

"Then they dragged me by the hair of my head to a police car. They didn't put me in the car then. They left me out on the ground to give others a chance to abuse me.

"Then they took me to the emergency room, and when I started to get out of the car, they grabbed me by the hair on my head and pulled me out on the concrete and drug me by my feet into the hospital and down the hall to a room and then threw me on a table."

The judge excused the witness and adjourned the jury for lunch. Of course, Judge Holland admonished the jury not to discuss the case with each other or with anyone else. But his admonishment didn't apply to the courtroom crowd, and anyone can imagine that those folks had a lot to say about Swindler's testimony. "If it was true, he deserved it," was the refrain opined over and over by the crowd of observers.

CHAPTER THIRTY

After the lunch break, Swindler was cross-examined by Prosecutor Karr, who was able to ask about his previous dealings with the law, but he could only go back ten years in his examination, which included arson, armed robbery, using a vehicle without the owner's permission, escaping from prison, and interstate transportation of a stolen vehicle. He had been found guilty of carrying a dangerous weapon, a thirteen-inch piece of steel, while in prison in Leavenworth.

Attorney Don Langston was able to question his client in a re-direct examination.

> Q. Now, you stated that the reason you carried weapons was because you had had some problems before. Had you ever shot at any officers before?
>
> A. No sir, I haven't. But I've been shot at.
>
> Q. Anything else that the officers and other police had done to you?
>
> A. Yes, sir.

Q. What have they done?

A. Well, in Pennsylvania when I was arrested about a stolen vehicle, I had no violence on my record at that time and it was publicized at that time that I was armed and dangerous, you see, and the only thing it was a stolen motor vehicle. They tried to force me off the road with a helicopter and there was shots fired to an extent of, at the time when the car was run off the road and I managed to get away on foot and I went into this house, I was completely surrounded by police that abused me pretty bad by threatening me with guns and what-have-you and so yes sir, police have been pretty bad by misusing their authority with guns.

Q. Did they give you some mental evaluation?

A. I spent 16 days there in the mental evaluation.

Q. Did they give you some—

A. So, when I went before the judge, the judge said to me, the reason why that I have done it, each one of them I have a reason and a set reason within my own mind for which I've been charged. I was cheated out of a will. I worked for a man for five years, A. E. Edwards, then as this Anna Edwards was his wife, and Mrs. Olive Edwards was his sister, Mrs. Hanna Edwards was his sister. So when he passed away of a heart attack—Now all of them was partial disabled but before hand he had told my grandmother and my mother to the effect if you let your son work for me, you know, I can't afford to pay him outrageous price, but if you see to it, you know, that he works for me and helps take care of me and what-have-you that will be, being I have no children of my own, I will treat him like a son and leave him a substantial, you know, so in dollars, in South Carolina he owned a little country house and a piece of property and that and several things that was supposed to be left to me, like a truck, a station wagon, for which his wife couldn't use it because she couldn't drive. She had this enormous home in town. All right, now on her death was supposed to be the understanding that I would also receive this, you see. So, when he passed away, they cheated me out of it, you see, and they got up there and well, they even tried to put it up in court for which I couldn't because we were poor and lived out in the country and at that time my father was in the State Hospital in Augusta, Georgia and—not in the State Hospital , but Veteran's Hospital in Augusta, Georgia. And with a nervous breakdown and a stroke also, and he was just not able to carry it to court so I lost out on it through flim-flam or through my last name like Swindler, like swindling somebody out of something.

Q. So this kind of thing forms in your mind over a period of time, is that what you mean?

A. If someone does you damage, I said I had a memory like an elephant, I can remember from now on. And if someone does damage to you, then—

Q. How do you feel about those events that transpired out there at that Conoco Service Station?

A. Well, I believe that the man was trying to get a bigger medal than what he got for simple reason he just come up and shot me. I have no idea what happened, Mr. Langston. It happened so fast. I can't explain it.

Q. Do you wish this hadn't happened?

A. You betcha. I wish it hadn't happened.

Q. Are you sorry about the officer?

A. I'm sorry that the whole thing happened. I certainly am. But I mean, that don't bring back a man's life because you're sorry that you just completely took it.

Q. But you wish it hadn't happened?

A. Yes, I do.

With that final response, the witness was excused. And the judge ruled that the court was in recess.

All that was left were the closing arguments.

When each attorney concluded, Judge Holland sent the jurors home around three p.m. He told them to come back on Saturday morning prepared to decide Swindler's fate.

On the following day, it didn't take long for the jury to come to a decision: guilty of capital murder. They were to decide later that day what his punishment would be. After five hours, the foreman of the jury, Charles Presley, told the judge that the decision of the jury was that Swindler should receive the death sentence by electrocution.

The judge then polled the jurors and asked each one if that was his or her decision. Several women jurors seemed on the verge of tears. One woman juror said, "He showed no remorse."

Judge Holland then asked Swindler to stand, and he was told that he would be sentenced to die by electrocution six weeks from the date of sentencing. Swindler said he planned to appeal, which actually was a formality according to Arkansas law.

Randy Basnett's spunky little wife, Cindy, mother of three, walked over to Charles Karr and hugged his neck.

The next morning the sheriff of Sebastian County drove Swindler to Cummins Prison in Grady, Arkansas, just outside Pine Bluff. There, he would await his fate.

CHAPTER THIRTY-ONE

Carl and Ruth Tinder said goodbye to their hideout on 10th and B at the Holiday Inn. They were ready to be in their pleasant living room and sit in familiar chairs. They liked to read the Sunday newspaper while sipping their morning coffee, made perfect in Ruth's old percolator she'd been given as a wedding present.

They were anxious to sleep in their own bed with its comfortable sheets and antique quilts sewn by relatives of Ruth's. No longer would they have to hear strange voices of motel guests checking in and becoming alarmed that it could be some of Swindler's thugs.

The policemen who had stayed in their living room and guarded them before they had to leave their home were nice men, but Ruth preferred to take off her hose and girdle and dress clothes as soon as she got home from work and put on her favorite seersucker house dress. She couldn't do that with the policemen there.

And next door, the Rivaldo kids returned to their familiar habits of talking on the phone, watching TV, having friends over for slumber parties, and taking snacks from the kitchen into their bedrooms. Their mom and dad contentedly settled into the noisy house they had missed while their kids were gone. When they climbed into their four-poster bed, Mary Rivaldo breathed a sigh of happiness. "Isn't that the loveliest of sounds?" she said to her husband as they listened to laughter coming from their daughters' bedroom. She waited for a response from her husband, but he had already fallen into peaceful sleep.

CHAPTER THIRTY-TWO

The lawmen of Columbia, South Carolina, surmised that the revolver used to kill Dottie and Greg was the same one Swindler used to kill Basnett. They asked that Arkansas send the revolver to Columbia so they could use it in their trial.

Neither Arkansas nor South Carolina wanted to take any chances of losing the gun. Sam Frierson, an Arkansas State Law Enforcement officer personally delivered the revolver to South Carolina and then returned it to Arkansas, preserving the chain of evidence.

Cindy flew to Columbia to attend Swindler's trial. She stayed close to the courthouse and walked to the trial each day. She paid for her own transportation and lodging, explaining to her dad that she did not begrudge spending the money.

She sat with Fort Smith police officers who were friends of Randy's and, during a recess in the South Carolina courtroom, she confronted Swindler and looked him in the eye. "Remember what I look like", she snarled, "because I'm going to follow you until you're dead. Don't forget what I look like. I'll always wear my hair just like I'm wearing it now."

Such moxie for such a little lady.

Cindy felt sorry for the parents of the couple killed. Swindler showed no remorse, which might have made the parents feel a little bit better. Of course, the parents wanted to know why.

Swindler admitted in trial that he had sodomized Greg and shot both him and his girlfriend in the head. The South Carolina jury found him guilty of capital murder, but he would be returned promptly to Arkansas. "We want him out of here," the prosecutor said. "Arkansas gets first dibs on him."

However, the governor of Arkansas, David Pryor, had ruled that there would be no electrocutions in Arkansas until the U. S. Supreme Court ruled for or against the death penalty. Besides that, the electric chair at the Arkansas prison had been dismantled and had not been used for ten years.

Furthermore, the Arkansas Supreme Court ruled that the defendant didn't receive a fair trial because of too much publicity, and that Judge Holland should have agreed to move the trial to another county. This ruling didn't take into account that Arkansas is a small state with a small population, and that most of the surrounding town folks watched television and subscribed to the Fort Smith newspapers and thus read the same news accounts that the city of Fort Smith residents did. Many folks who lived in surrounding counties worked in Fort Smith because that was where the employment opportunities were.

Nevertheless, the new trial for Swindler would be in Waldron, the county seat of Scott County, which was far away from Fort Smith but still in an adjoining judicial district.

Judge Dave Partain would be the judge presiding over the second trial. The new trial was set for October 16, 1978. Swindler would be imprisoned in Fort Smith and transferred each day to Waldron.

Judge Partain resided in Van Buren, a town east of Fort Smith. He was a handsome man with a slow Southern drawl who had been a bachelor for many years before he married a beautiful woman, Norma. They had a daughter, Paige. Her father, who was almost old enough to be her grandfather, adored her.

When the trial officially started, it seemed that it would be impossible to find twelve people who had not already decided that Swindler was guilty. The new trial was expensive, and Judge Partain's office members didn't like the drive each day. Nor did the prosecuting attorneys or the defense attorneys.

CHAPTER THIRTY-THREE

Swindler griped about his accommodations at the county jail, saying it was the worst jail he'd ever been in, and that his rights were being denied. His food was cold. His coffee was cold. There was no available cool water for him to drink. He couldn't worship Satan; thus, he was being denied his right to religious freedom. He wasn't allowed to exercise. He pissed and moaned constantly and made threats to the jailers and sometimes other prisoners.

He often was asked for interviews by local newspapers and television stations in the area. He was hot news, and he enjoyed the notoriety. He told reporters that he had no remorse about anything. He grew up where guns "was as common as clothes."

While Swindler was waiting at the Sebastian County Jail for his second trial to begin, he tried to engage in conversation with other inmates and jail workers. In one brief conversation he found out that one of the jailers, Nilo "Chico" Acosta, was from Key West, Florida. He tried to engage Acosta in longer conversations, and once he did, he asked Acosta to see if he could get him a Florida newspaper that would have been published around the first of January, 1976.

Acosta told Swindler that he'd see what he could do. "Why do you want to see that newspaper?" he asked.

"Well, I want to read about a murder that took place. I left a body down there."

Acosta could tell by the smirk on Swindler's face and the gleam in his eyes, that he should report this conversation to the sheriff. He knew that some prisoners made up stories to enhance their reputation as a really bad guy, but others just liked to brag about their feats.

The sheriff of Sebastian County called several Florida sheriffs' departments and hit bingo. On January tenth, 1976, a badly decomposed body was discovered in an abandoned real estate shack on Lower Matecumbe Key.

Swindler's fingerprints were sent to the Florida sheriff, and those were compared to a fingerprint found on a cereal box under the body. It was a match.

The body was a University of Pittsburgh nineteen-year-old student named Jeffrey McNerney who had been to Florida with friends to scuba dive. However, he didn't like the area and the place where he and his friends were camping, so he left to hitchhike to his aunt's house in Fort Lauderdale. His friends would pick him up on their way home to Pennsylvania.

He had never hitchhiked before.

A nice couple with children first picked up Jeffrey, but they dropped him off after fifteen miles. He once again stuck out his thumb and was soon picked up by Swindler. Jeffrey told him that he was a college student who was in Florida with some friends and was headed to his aunt's house.

Swindler didn't like college kids. Since Columbia was home to the University of South Carolina, he had been around college students in lots of places, especially bars. They always treated him like something on the bottom of their shoes.

Swindler took Jeffrey to a deserted real estate shack, where he tied him to a metal-framed bed. He tied both hands to the head of the bed and tied his right foot to the bottom of the bed. He savagely violated the boy over several days.

When he was through with Jeffrey, he smashed his head with a twenty-five-pound pickax and left him there. He had been dead ten days when he was discovered. The authorities had no clue except for a fingerprint left on a cereal box they found under the bed.

Of course, his family knew he was missing because he never showed up at his aunt's house. One can only imagine the agony his family suffered, and then when their son was discovered, they had to live with what they knew were their son's last days.

When this happened, Swindler had been on parole from prison and staying at a halfway house in South Carolina. He left by means of elaborate lies, but he was later caught and back he went to prison in South Carolina. Nobody connected him to the brutal crime that took place in Florida.

CHAPTER THIRTY-FOUR

The second trial began on October 16, 1977, and 153 people showed up for the jury pool. Judge Partain hoped three days would be sufficient to pick a jury. It wasn't easy because nearly all the possible jurors admitted reading about Swindler and the death of Randy Basnett. They also watched the news on television. It was slow going, but finally a jury of nine men and three women was chosen. It had taken five days to find twelve people who had not already formed an opinion about the case.

Swindler's attorney, Don Langston, continually filed motions to change the charge to first degree murder, move the trial, or declare a mistrial. Judge Partain ruled against all of Langston's motions.

The second trial was not much different than the first trial. Carl Tinder, Steve Cardwell, and Charles Lambert testified as eye witnesses who saw Swindler's murder of Randy Basnett. Police officers testified about the capture of Swindler down in the river bottoms where a thick bunch of trees and brush grew.

Although Swindler claimed that he was roughed up by the lawmen who captured him, none of the policemen called as witnesses admitted to seeing him beaten. Bob Ross said he feared Swindler was making a move

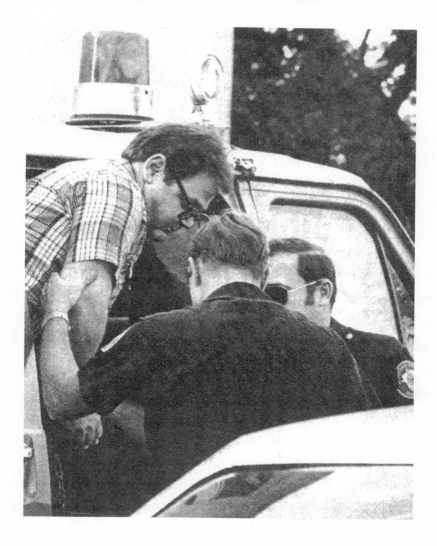

A slimmed-down and short-haired Swindler arrives in Waldron, Arkansas, for his second trial for the murder of Randy Basnett.

to escape, so he hit him with the butt end of his shotgun. When asked why, Bob Ross declared, "I'm only human. Swindler killed one of my best friends. I didn't want to take a chance of him getting away."

Cindy and her dad attended the second trial. Her plan was to stare him down and make him uncomfortable. It worked because he kept complaining to his attorney that she was bothering him. He wanted his attorney to tell the judge to kick her out of the courtroom.

Of course, Cindy could tell that she was accomplishing what she set out to do. She watched him turn his head to see if she was still staring at him. Hurrah, she thought, I'm making him squirm.

Swindler received the same guilty verdict in Waldron as he did in Fort Smith. He was clearly a man who would kill again if he were ever released into society. The sentence would be appealed, and because of that he'd have at least a year before dying in the electric chair.

It seemed to Cindy that the radio and television stations reported on Swindler's court proceedings daily. Her children would be watching a television show when it would be interrupted about Swindler's various court cases.

On a popular radio station, KISR, which played the top hits of the day, the owner and announcer, Fred Baker, announced that a True Detective magazine was on sale at a local magazine business, and screamed "You Better Get 'Em While They're Hot." She learned later that the magazine had sent journalists and photographers to cover her husband's funeral. There was a picture in the magazine of her hugging one of Randy's friends.

This so incensed Cindy that she called on her friend and attorney, Jack Rose, to get the announcement off the air. Instead, he went to the establishment and bought all the available copies.

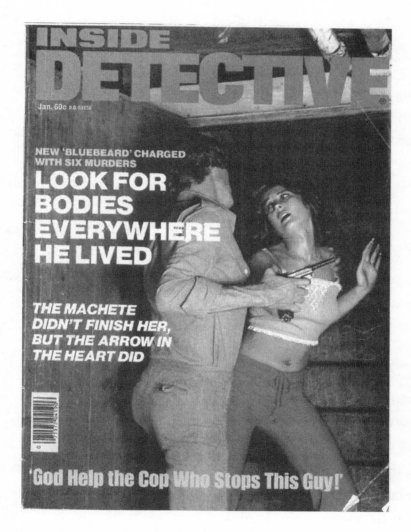

Inside Detective magazine with accounts of the murder of Randy Basnett.

Even though Fort Smith was her home, Cindy thought more and more about selling her house in Barling and moving to Tahlequah, Oklahoma, where Lake Tenkiller was located. After all, her parents now lived there, and her husband had always dreamed of living at the Lake. She thought she would feel close to Randy there. And sure enough, whenever she visited her parents at the lake, she often heard his voice when a thunder cloud suddenly appeared: "Everybody to the house!" he always yelled to his family.

Randy and most other fishermen believed that lightning was drawn to water. He had known of several people struck by lightning when they were fishing. There were little coves that fishermen could find to seek shelter. These were little dark, quiet spots where the water was still and beautiful. Randy had often taken Cindy to those coves for romantic moments.

She and her parents together purchased a large four-bedroom manufactured home built specifically for them by a company in Tulsa. It was moved onto the land her parents already owned.

There, in 1981, five years after Randy's death, Cindy and her children found paradise.

Her mother planted iris all around the home, and her dad built a circle drive and planted shrubbery and trees. There was plenty of space in which the children could play. Wildlife surrounded them: deer, wild turkey, geese, rabbits. They watched out a window while does and their fawns appeared in their back yard. There was the beauty of nature, with the morning sun sparkling down on the lake. Sometimes, Cindy imagined she saw Randy fishing. Sometimes the sight of a man who looked like Randy made her cry. But as months whiled away, and she saw an image that reminded her of her husband, she didn't cry. Instead, she smiled and pointed out the scene to her children.

Cindy and her children were happy living in the vicinity of laughter and thrills of caught catfish, bass, and crappie. They enjoyed watching the water skiers do their stuff. They eventually made friends with the locals, and no radio or television ever rang out the name of John Swindler.

Swindler granted interviews to reporters who asked for them. He clearly enjoyed his fame. He wanted sympathy: Swindler had been fat and teased at school. Consequently, he didn't like school and set out many mornings for his usual walk to elementary school, only to take a different route to a serene part of the forest where taunts weren't screamed at him. And often, if he did make it to school on time, when the bell rang at the end of the day, Swindler chased classmates home with a knife in his hand.

His mother had blamed the other children in his school, as well as the teachers, for teasing him about being dumb and fat. He weighed two hundred pounds in the fourth grade, and he soon dropped out of elementary school and never properly learned to read or write.

Swindler said he received terrible head injuries when he fell from a bridge as a child. He said that fall was the beginning of his trouble. His mother was also real fat, weighing close to three hundred pounds. She was mean, he said, and had his father committed to a mental hospital. Of course, Swindler lied when he testified in court that his mother taught Sunday school. And he never sang in a choir.

He was housed on death row at Cummins State Prison in Grady, Arkansas. Like others there, he was waiting for his death sentence to be carried out.

Cindy found a perverse feeling of happiness by calling the warden at Cummins Prison two or three times a week to ask how Swindler was doing.

"Did he have any visitors?"

"Has he been sick?"

"Is he still fat?"

She carried on for three years until her father convinced her that it was not healthy to torment the warden with her phone calls.

And, by this time, the Florida authorities knew that he had killed the young man from Pennsylvania. They brought him to Florida where he was questioned. He knew the jailer, Acosta, had turned him in. Acosta was fearful that Swindler would somehow retaliate.

Florida authorities wished they could have brought him to trial first. He was actually scheduled for trial there three different times, but appeals kept arising. The Florida governor wrote to the Arkansas governor often, each trying to figure out how to handle this horrible problem that had fallen in their lap. A man can only be executed once.

Jeff McNerney's father was quoted as saying Jeff had never hitchhiked in his life and was not street smart. He should have been leery of getting into a car with a man who looked like Swindler, but he had been totally without prejudice concerning someone's looks. He had been a well-built young man of 5 ft. 7 inches and weighed 150 pounds. He was a champion swimmer and had won swimming trophies galore. He was just Swindler's type.

Swindler was later charged with the crime in Florida and made his first court appearance on August 27, 1982. Mr. McNerney went to Florida three times to see Swindler's scheduled trials, but through legal maneuvering of asking for a speedy trial, Swindler avoided prosecution.

Jeff McNerney, a champion swimmer and honor student, before brutally murdered and left tied to an iron bed on New Year's Day in 1976.

Mr. McNerney and Cindy Basnett corresponded by mail and telephone, each feeling some kind of bond because of what Swindler had done to their loved one.

Swindler was returned to Cummins State Prison in Grady, Arkansas, which was close to Little Rock, to await the date of his death for the murder of a Fort Smith policeman.

Since Swindler had also been found guilty in the South Carolina trial for his murders of the young couple in Columbia, he hoped he could spend his last days in the prison facilities of South Carolina, which were much more agreeable to him than those in Arkansas. But Arkansas had tried him first, so they got to kill him first.

Swindler tried hard to become a model prisoner. He lost weight, cut his hair, and learned to read and write. He even taught other prisoners the basics.

He also requested comfort be administrated to him by Monsignor John O'Donnell, whom he had met thirteen years earlier when O'Donnell was a priest in Fort Smith. At that time, Swindler had a long, thick beard and had worshipped Satan.

The priest didn't believe in the death penalty, and, of course, Swindler told the priest he no longer worshiped Satan.

O'Donnell realized Swindler had become fastidious with his appearance. Even in prison clothes, he kept his shirt tucked into his pants. Always clean-shaven, with his hair shampooed and cut short, he appeared to be a model citizen of the prison.

Father O'Donnell called Swindler an enigma. Because the priest couldn't figure him out, he gave Swindler the benefit of the doubt. Of course, Swindler told the priest he was sorry for his crimes and wanted forgiveness for his sins. The priest and other Catholics launched a campaign to ask for clemency for Swindler, thus saving him from death. A group of Catholic women wrote letters beseeching the clemency board to save this man from the electric chair.

Others called Swindler a fraud, as well as a cold-blooded killer who had never asked forgiveness until he was able to con a popular, good-looking priest in Little Rock, the capital of Arkansas. (It was no secret that Little Rock folks thought of Fort Smith as second-class.)

John Mohnhaupt, a former Arkansas prison guard, testified to a parole board that was considering clemency for Swindler. He told about Swindler's reading material, which consisted of books on survival, how to live off the land when he escaped from prison, how to kill people more efficiently, and munitions catalogs.

Mohnhaupt also said the worst duty he ever had was being locked in the gymnasium with Swindler once a week when he was supposed to exercise. "He wouldn't do anything but sit down and tell me how great it was to kill people. He has crazy eyes and when he talked about his methods for killing people, he'd laugh and laugh."

Sebastian County Prosecuting Attorney Ron Fields drove down to Little Rock from Fort Smith to tell the board that the death penalty was the only way to keep Swindler from killing again. "If he is incarcerated the rest of his life, there's no guarantee he will stay in prison."

Others spoke in favor of carrying out the death penalty. One was the jailer, Chico Acosta. He seemed almost frightened telling the board about his conversations with Swindler. Swindler had asked Acosta to get a newspaper from the Key West area around January of 1976 for him so he could read about himself.

"I left a body down there," he had boasted.

When the Florida authorities arrived at Fort Smith to interview

Swindler, he was surprised. "Chico," he said to me, "You're cold blooded."

Later, when Swindler was getting ready to be transferred to a maximum prison in Grady, Arkansas, he asked to see Acosta.

"He said he wanted to shake my hand, so we shook hands through the bars. Then he said, 'I want you to know that if I ever escape and see you on the street and I have weapons or guns, that I won't kill you. I know you were doing your job.'"

Acosta also remembered: "He asked me to write down my address, so he could send me a Christmas card. Of course, I wouldn't give it to him."

But Swindler did write to Acosta a few times in care of the Sebastian County Jail. He sent one Christmas card to him that he had drawn a picture of a man with only half a head, with blood dripping down and the words, drip, splash.

"He loved to talk about murder and guns, and when he did, he'd get this gleam in his eyes and a smirk on his lips. He was weird. He was a really weird guy."

His victims' families wrote letters or appeared in person, begging the board not to even consider clemency for Swindler.

One particularly poignant letter came from Jeffrey McNerney's father. It was addressed to Mr. Mike Gaines who was Chairman of State Board of Parole and Criminal Rehabilitation.

Dear Mr. Gaines,

Please let me introduce myself. My name is Joseph F. McNerney, the father of Jeffrey C. McNerney who was murdered on or about January 1, 1976, on Lower Matecumbe Key by John Edward Swindler.

By his own admission, Mr. Swindler was at the scene and responsible for my son's death. Mr. Swindler's fingerprint was also found at the scene and identified.

As a result of pre-trial publicity and legal maneuvering on the part of Mr. Swindler and his counsel, the statute of a speedy trial was running out, and therefore, an agreement was made between the Governors of Florida and Arkansas to return him to Arkansas and receive the sentence for the murder of Police Officer Randy Basnett.

We know this man has murdered four persons, kidnapped and robbed three others and shot and robbed another. This man is aware of his crimes and holds no remorse for his actions. Anyone knowing this man feels if he had the opportunity, he would kill again. I feel there is nothing mentally wrong with this man other than he is a killer and enjoys killing anyone.

Please, I beg of you, carry out the sentence he was given. The families of the victims need to feel some relief even though their loved ones will never return. They will have some satisfaction that Mr. Swindler will no longer harm anyone. This man has been tried and convicted and found guilty of capital first degree murder in Arkansas and given the death sentence. It has now been fourteen years, and he has used every maneuver possible to avoid his death sentence. Every avenue has been exhausted, and the sentence is to be carried out on June 18, 1990.

Please do not delay his just due any longer.

Yours very truly,

Joseph McNerney

CHAPTER THIRTY-FIVE

Swindler had already chosen to die in the prison's new electric chair, probably because it was a most sensational news story. He was scheduled to die on Monday, June 18 at 9:00 p.m., 1990, unless Governor Bill Clinton reduced the sentence to life without parole.

Randy's mother, Peggy Basnett, told a reporter with Little Rock's Arkansas Gazette newspaper, "If it happens, we'll be thrilled, but we won't believe it till it happens. After waiting some fourteen years for Swindler's death sentence to be carried out, we're not ruling out some last-minute delay."

Peggy Basnett said they would be waiting by the telephone in Fort Smith at their son Bill's house on Monday night, June 18th. "If it does happen, then maybe we can get back to normal. We'll still miss Randy, but maybe I'll never have to hear Swindler's name again, or see his face."

Governor Clinton was Swindler's last hope. The governor met with Cindy Basnett, and she was forceful in her demands that the man who killed her husband be electrocuted. "That's what two juries said to do," she told him.

Clinton declined to grant clemency. It was a decision hailed by many people.

Swindler refused to choose a last meal. Instead he magnanimously chose to have what the other prisoners were having, which was barbeque chicken, rice and gravy, pinto beans, early June peas, fresh squash and peaches, hot rolls, and milk.

He was quoted as saying, "I'm not afraid to die, and I wouldn't admit it if I was."

CHAPTER THIRTY-SIX

Swindler asked his champion, Msgr. O'Donnell, to stay with him until the appointed hour of execution.

Swindler dictated a statement to O'Donnell to be read to the media after his execution. It read, "I have no animosity toward anyone. I hold no grudge. I appreciate the care and love others have shown me and the other people on death row. I thank the Diocese of Little Rock for my arrangements and my last requests that will be carried out. I hope this brings to light the injustice of capital punishment and the need to abolish it."

Linda Seubold, a popular journalist in Fort Smith, witnessed the electrocution and reported on it for the Fort Smith newspaper. She wrote:

"Swindler was already strapped in the high-backed wooden chair when the black curtains were opened. The ten witnesses were shielded by four Plexiglas windows. His naturally red, fleshy face was covered with a brown leather mask that exposed only his bulbous nose and ample chin. He was dressed in a two-piece white prison uniform. His right leg was exposed from the top of his white sock to his knee where his pant leg had been pulled up to accommodate the electrodes attached to his right calf. Swindler did not answer when he was asked if he had a last statement.

"A click was heard and the resulting jolt pressed Swindler back against the chair. The fingers of both hands were tightly clenched over his thumbs. His toes were curled inside his socks. His head was tilted back, and at one point a clear fluid trickled down the left side of his mask. At 9:04 the faint hum that could be heard when the switch was thrown had stopped and Swindler's body slumped in the chair."

Linda Seubold and Cindy had become acquainted over the years since Randy's death. Cindy and her uncle, Howard Moss, a former policeman who lived in Little Rock, were planning to witness the execution, but Cindy changed her mind and didn't attend. Ironically, the date of Swindler's execution was also the birthday of Amanda Basnett, Randy's daughter who was only three months old when he was murdered by Swindler.

Seubold knew of Cindy's change of plans, so she called Cindy at her uncle's house in Little Rock after the execution was over. Sensing that the execution had bothered Seubold more than she was willing to admit, Cindy invited Seubold and her photographer to spend the night in Little Rock at her uncle's home. The next morning they sat out on a deck and visited. Their visit was later reported on in the Southwest Times Record under the headline of Widow Reminisces.

Cindy told Seubold that Amanda, the daughter who was only three months old when her father was killed, was a typical teenager. She had the same disposition and attitude and cockiness as her dad. They both loved to play and, as a child, Randy had never wanted to come in for supper. "They both would rather play than eat."

Cindy also remembered the time she was invited to Kimmons Junior High in Fort Smith. They presented her a plaque to honor her husband. "Randy would visit the school and talk to the students. He built up a good friendship there."

She said that two policeman friends of Randy's escorted her to the school to receive the plaque. "When I walked into the gym, the entire student body stood up."

Another example of Randy's rapport with teens came in the form of a letter. It was written by a teenage boy who was stopped by Officer Basnett for violation of curfew. The boy was already on a bad path, but Randy talked to him and the next day dropped by to see him. The teenager had read about his death, and he wanted his widow to know how her husband had encouraged him to be a better citizen.

Father O'Donnell, who became Swindler's advocate for life in prison instead of the death penalty.

CHAPTER THIRTY-SEVEN

On the night of Swindler's death, at 9:04 on Monday night, June 18, 1990, a group of anti-capital punishment protesters had gathered around the prison area under a shade tree to pray for Swindler, his victims, all the families involved, and all the people in the state of Arkansas.

On the other side of the road, an estimated fifty people, including Fort Smith policemen, held up signs of electric chairs with the words, "Burn, Baby, Burn." Two young women gleefully danced at the news that Swindler was dead. His body was transferred to a funeral home in Little Rock in a long, black hearse.

Msgr. O'Donnell told the press that Swindler had asked that the Catholic Church claim his body and his ashes be buried the next day at Little Rock's Calvary Cemetery in a plot donated by St. Joseph's Church.

Nobody in Swindler's family wanted his body. His brother, Robert, who had met him at the Columbia, South Carolina, bus station after he was released from Leavenworth, told reporters that when John got out of prison the first time, his whole personality had changed. He was a hardened criminal from then on. "He chose his path, and he had to pay the consequences."

EPILOGUE

Cindy was happy with her decision to move to Oklahoma. Her children attended schools there and performed well in the classroom. Her oldest children graduated from Tahlequah High School. Shannon married a man who eventually became a high school coach there. Her youngest, Amanda, graduated high school from Southside High School after spending the school months with her paternal grandparents in Fort Smith.

After Cindy's beloved father died, she and her mother decided enough years had passed that it might be time to move back to Fort Smith. Cindy's mom had heart problems, and all her doctors were in Fort Smith. Without a whole lot of planning, they put their home up for sale. It sold quickly before they had a chance to decide where they would move to in Fort Smith.

Cindy had laughed with her mother when they realized they had failed to remember her dad's rule of the Six P's: Prior Planning Prevents Piss-Poor Performance.

However, Cindy and her mom found a cute duplex to rent in south Fort Smith.

Cindy never remarried, and she has remained in the same duplex for thirty-eight years. Her and Randy's daughter, Amanda, as a young mother, developed a heart condition. After many trips to the Arkansas Heart Hospital in Little Rock with Cindy, she died at the age of thirty-five.

Cindy consoled herself by believing her husband would be teaching his daughter how to fish. Up in heaven.

— The End—

Dear Readers,
If you enjoyed this
book enough to review
it for Goodreads, B&N,
or Amazon.com, I'd
appreciate it!
Thanks, Anita

Find more great reads at
Pen-L.com

Acknowledgements

Thanks for encouragement and help from:
Dixie Kline, Marla Cantrell, Marcus Coker, Christina
Scherrey, Eleanor Clark, Alan and Debbie Foliart,
and my beloved sister, Mary Pratt.

And especially for Cindy Basnett,
whose prayers allowed me to write this book.

About Anita

I suppose one can say I've had two sepa-
rate lives. Twenty-six years ago, I became a
widow and overnight went from being a wife
who longed to be a writer to a widow who
needed a job. I jumped at a chance to become
manager of a Fort Smith, Arkansas, branch
library. Though I no longer had a partner who
encouraged my dreams, the customers in the
Miller Branch Library became my friends
and eased the pain of widowhood. As I've said many times, "The
library saved my life."

After almost sixteen years, I reluctantly retired due to a bad hip I call
"an old football injury." A dear friend who owned a bookstore suggested
I get back into my writing life. Her encouraging words were, "You're a lot
better writer now than you used to be."

I knew the book I'd write: a true story about a crime that took place
in my hometown of Van Buren, Arkansas. I'd tried to write the story in
different forms from the age of thirty-six on. This new version took a couple of years in the making, and what became Blind Rage a popular true
crime novel was published by Pen-L Publishing in 2015. Two successful
true-crime novels have followed, Closing Time and Cold Blooded, and I'm
delighted to say I now have a tribe of readers to keep me company.

Closing Time

A true story of robbery and ruthless double murder that shook a small town.

Kenneth Staton was the well-respected owner of a jewelry store in Van Buren, Arkansas. Although crippled with rheumatoid arthritis and unable to walk without crutches, he had built his business through excellent watch repair work, fine quality jewelry sold at fair prices, and a dedication to his customers that surpassed all other merchants. He was the quintessential gentleman in all aspects of his life, and a beloved father.

Unknown to him, two men—a seasoned criminal with a propensity for violence and a younger man, handsome, but broke and with an obsessive thirst for alcohol—plotted to rob the jewelry store at closing time on September 10, 1980. The thugs had only met each other days before, and it was the younger one's first venture into armed robbery.

When Staton and his daughter Suzanne didn't show up for supper, his other two daughters became alarmed and went to the store. There they found the bodies of their father and youngest sister lying in pools of blood, gagged, hogtied, and shot twice in the head. Close to $100,000 dollars in diamonds and other jewelry had been stolen.

This senseless, bloody crime rocked the town of Van Buren and set its lawmen, sworn to find the killers, on a fiercely determined hunt that led from Rogers, Arkansas to Jacksonville, Florida, and all the way to Vancouver, Canada.

Seventeen years later, was justice served?

Cold Blooded

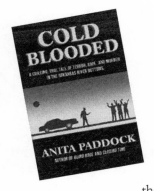

**A chilling, true tale of terror, rape and murder
in the Arkansas River bottoms.**

On a cold January morning in 1981, a knock on an apartment door began what would become one of the bloodiest crime sprees in Arkansas history.

In the coming days the bodies of newlyweds Larry and Jawana Price, businessman Holly Gentry, and Police Detective Ray Tate were discovered. They had been executed in cold blood and discarded like so much trash.

What kind of person murders four people in cold blood?

Did the right one go to prison?